Class of '63

Class of '63

The extraordinary, revealing and heroic stories of
15 men ordained as Catholic priests 40 years ago

COMPILED AND EDITED BY
TONY CASTLE

kevin
mayhew

First published in 2003 by
KEVIN MAYHEW LTD
Buxhall, Stowmarket, Suffolk, IP14 3BW
E-mail: info@kevinmayhewltd.com
KINGSGATE PUBLISHING INC
1000 Pannell Street, Suite G, Columbia, MO 65201
E-mail: sales@kingsgatepublishing.com

9 8 7 6 5 4 3 2 1 0

ISBN 1 84417 154 X
Catalogue No 1500644

Cover design by Angela Selfe
Typesetting by Richard Weaver

Printed and bound in Great Britain

Contents

Acknowledgements

The editor would like to express his gratitude to the following for their kind assistance: Mr Michael Kennedy, Diocesan Chancery Administrator of the Archdiocese of Southwark, for his support and material on Father Kenneth Snaith; and Monsignor Canon John Hull, vicar-general of the Arundel and Brighton Diocese, for putting me in touch with James Wilson and for his assistance with material on Father Stephen Hinde, which included putting me in touch with Stephen's sister, Clemency Hinde, who kindly provided additional material. A 'thank you' is due to Canon James Pannett, Canon James Cronin and Canon John McNamara for help and advice. Each of the contributors would like to thank those who, like Ann Smiley of Our Lady of Ransom, Eastbourne, helped in any way with typing, and so forth.

The class of '63 would collectively and publicly like to express their gratitude to Peter and Paulette Coldham and their family for their generous and loving care of Ken Bell for over 20 years; and equally to Doreen Bergin and family for the same generosity in their unselfish loving care of Joe Ware.

*Dedicated to the memory of Stephen Hinde (1984)
Kenneth Snaith (1991) and John Medcalf (2002)*

*'May we meet one day merrily in heaven'
(St Thomas More)*

From the left Back Row: Richard Quinlan, John Medcalf, Michael Ivers, James Wilson, Sean O'Callaghan, Stephen Hinde, Kenneth Bell *Front Row:* Joseph Ware, Kevin Pelham, Kenneth Snaith, (Mgr Iggleden, rector), Anthony Castle, Anthony Shelley, David Payne

Introduction

This is a unique and timely book. In June 1963, fifteen men, most of whom were in their mid-twenties and thus the last of the prewar babies, prostrated themselves before their bishop and generously dedicated the rest of their lives to the service of Christ. In the southeast of England they were the first Catholic priests of a new age. The Second Vatican Council era had just dawned and these new priests, trained under the old dispensation were to live out their ministries amid the changes, challenges and uncertainties of the new dispensation. This book is unique for it records how those young men coped, adapted and followed their consciences in a difficult and turbulent period in the history of their Church.

It is a timely book for, in the last few years, the Catholic priest-hood has been through a disturbing period and a new experience. The behaviour of a tiny minority of the clergy has cast a shadow over all and in some quarters has occasioned a loss of confidence in the priesthood. This record of the last 40 years paints a totally different picture. Here, simply and sincerely expressed (and the secular clergy are not accustomed to writing publicly about themselves) are accounts which reveal that the Christian virtues of deep faith and faithfulness, unselfish service and dedication, courage and commitment are truly alive and well among our parish clergy.

Thirteen of the men who had trained for six years together at St John's Seminary, Wonersh, were ordained in the college chapel on 8 June by their bishop, Monsignor Cyril Cowderoy of Southwark. That same Pentecost, in Ireland, two other young men who had volunteered to work in the Southwark diocese were also ordained. Later that summer they arrived in London, reported their presence at Bishop's House, Southwark, and joined the Class of '63.

In each of the 20 dioceses of England and Wales that June there were ordinations, as there were throughout the thousands of dioceses that make up the Catholic Church. The particular group, whose history is celebrated here, is but a microcosm; each

The Diocesan Seminaries in the 1960s
for the Southwark Archdiocese

St Joseph's College, Mark Cross, Sussex

St John's Seminary, Wonersh, Guildford, Surrey

of the other groups, who were ordained 40 years ago, have their own, perhaps similar stories to tell. Together they provide a reassurance that, out of sight of the public gaze, the Catholic ordained ministry is faithfully making Christ present in the world.

The candidates for ordination in 1963 had been trained to celebrate the old Tridentine Mass in Latin, with their backs to the people, in and with a perfect liturgical rigidity. Within two years all that had changed, with little explanation and no preparation. But a greater shockwave hit them, in 1968, when their training in a disciplined lifestyle, accompanied by unquestioned respect for authority, was put to the test. Immersed in compassionate daily pastoral care they were confronted with the authoritative demands of *Humanae Vitae* (Pope Paul VI's letter on birth control, published on 28 July). Confusion reigned as all pastoral priests found themselves caught between the expectations of the laity and a hierarchy divided between bishops who expected unquestioned obedience and those who sought a gentler and more pastoral approach. That summer of 1968 was a very disturbing and painful time.

This is not the place to trace the struggle of conscience most clergy endured or the individual positions adopted by the Class of '63 (a full report of these times can be found in Owen Hardwicke's *Living Beyond Conformity*, Columba Press). Sufficient to say that three of the Class – Stephen Hinde, Michael Ivers and David Payne – felt sufficiently strongly about the issue to sign the famous letter to *The Times*, organised by Kenneth Allan, Nigel Collingwood and Peter de Rosa.

Adrian Hastings records in *A History of English Christianity* (Collins) that priests were caught between laity and bishops: they were in trouble publicly if they dissented from the encyclical, but of course they could say what they really thought privately and in confession. It was a demoralizing situation. Not many of its supporters actually argued for the infallible character of what the pope had said, and a sharp decline in respect for papal authority became evident.

A further unexpected event that shaped the lives of the new priests was the announcement, kept secret until the very last minute, that the large diocese of Southwark, for which they had been ordained, was splitting into two. On 28 May 1965 the new diocese of Arundel and Brighton came into existence. The clergy were given no choice, but simply informed that the place where they were serving on that day determined which diocese they now belonged to. Bishop Cashman was to lead the new diocese and in 1971, on his death, Mgr Michael Bowen took his place. In 1977 he was transferred to Southwark and was succeeded by Bishop Cormac Murphy O'Connor, later to follow Cardinal Basil Hume at Westminster.

The idea for this book took shape early in 2001. The first idea was for the editor to interview as many of the Class as could be contacted. These interviews took place but, on reflection, each priest wanted to use the interview script as the basis for his own account. This explains why the structure of each is similar – starting with the family background and the conviction of a vocation and so forth – but why each also has its own tone. There are two exceptions. Joe Ware's entry remains in the original interview form and so does John Medcalf's, because he died shortly afterwards.

Secular priests live for their parishes; that is what they are trained for and what gives their lives meaning and purpose. For this reason each account takes us through the parishes where the priest was sent by his bishop (in the early years there was no consultation or consideration given to the wishes of the priest, but that too has now changed).

The fifteen men who make up the Class of '63 fall into three groups. First we have the priests who are still faithfully and actively serving Christ and their people in the parishes of Carshalton Beeches, Eastbourne, Hailsham and Putney. Then come those who are retired or, sadly, deceased. Finally, there is the group of five, who, for several reasons, are no longer active in the ordained ministry.

Forty years after ordination, and having reached or passed the normal retirement age, means little or nothing to those still working in parishes. The work must, and will, go on while health and strength permits. In a world dominated by ambition, and not infrequently by rampant greed; in a society where most of the educated carve out a lucrative career for themselves and then look for a comfortable retirement in their fifties, these men are 'other worldly'. Their only ambition has been, for 40 years, to be faithful to their calling; to serve their people and through them, their God. The concept of 'career' has never entered their heads; they received a 'call' to ministry and they have done their best to respond to that call in the place and role directed by their bishop.

While this book is primarily and ostensibly a celebration of priesthood, the reader will not miss the considerable contribution made to these stories by the laity. One wonders, for example, what would have happened to Ken Bell and Joe Ware but for the unselfish and loving generosity of the Coldham and Bergin families. Then there is the deep faith and solid prayer-life of the parents, which was repeatedly shown to be the seedbed of these vocations and their support through many years of training. It was the laity that brought John Medcalf back to the active ministry and who similarly offered loving support to me. The constant and generous encouragement of innumerable parishioners, over the years, has sustained each priest in their story of service.

There are certain identifiable threads running through each story: the care and concern for youth, the interest and enthusiasm for ecumenism, and, repeatedly in every account, the importance of the role of the laity and the need to give more scope and responsibility to them. Gathered here, simply and directly put, are ideas and suggestions for the future of the Church that spring from many years of experience. They come from but a small sample of priests, but their hard work and dedication over 40 faithful years demand respect and attention.

Constantly in my mind as I called to see and work with the contributors while preparing this book, was the great privilege of being associated which such self-effacing and dedicated men. In their Ruby year they merit some recognition; *ad multos annos.*

TONY CASTLE

I
Background

Commencement

In early September 1957, 17 new students arrived at St John's Seminary, Wonersh, near Guildford in Surrey to commence their six years of preparation for the Catholic priesthood. Most were in their late teens or early twenties; a few were older and were conscious of being 'late vocations'. These included Kenneth Snaith, being the eldest at 34. He, like John Medcalf, was a convert to Catholicism. Both had prepared for Wonersh by spending a year or two at Osterley, a college run by the Jesuits in West London. Six had 'come up' from the junior seminary of St Joseph's, Mark Cross, in Sussex. One of the youngest of the group, Tony Castle, had spent six years at Mark Cross and because he was just about to commence his seventh year in seminaries he was the 'senior' of the Year.

The seminary was full (it was extended to take more students about three years later) and the new students were accommodated at the top of the building in narrow wooden cubicles with shared washing facilities. (They received proper rooms in their second year.) Academically they were just about to commence two years of Philosophy, with some Scripture and Church History. In the refectory they found that they were allocated places on tables of 10 to 12 students.

In alphabetical order they were: Kenneth Bell, Kevin Carroll, Anthony Castle*, Terence Earley*, Peter Elliott*, Stephen Hinde, Michael Ivers, John Medcalf, Sean O'Callaghan, David Payne, Kevin Pelham*, Frederick Phipps, Richard Quinlan*, Kenneth Snaith, Anthony Shelley*, Joseph Ware, James Wilson.

Three students – Terence Earley, Peter Elliott and Frederick Phipps – left the Class in 1958. Kevin Carroll left the following year.

Meanwhile in Ireland Patrick Moloney and Séamus Hester were commencing their six years at seminary. They joined the Class of '63 on their arrival in the Southwark diocese. (There was a third irish priest, who wishes to remain nameless, who declined the invitation to be included in this book.)

(* previously at Mark Cross)

Liturgical steps to the priesthood

In the 1950s and 1960s, before the liturgical reforms of the Second Vatican Council, there were six Orders to be received on the way to the priesthood, after the Tonsure. (The Tonsure conferred upon the candidate the rights and obligations of the clerical state.) First came the Minor Orders, which included Doorkeeper and Reader; then Second Minor Orders, which included Exorcist and Acolyte. A legally prescribed length of time had to elapse between each set of Orders and the candidate had to apply for each, some weeks beforehand. He knew if his application had been accepted when he was summoned to the Rector/President of the seminary, who would issue a 'call'. Orders could be, and were sometimes, deferred. The same rules applied to the two Major Orders of Subdeacon and Deacon. The whole process was reformed in the early 1970s.

The commitment to lifelong celibacy was made, at the Subdiaconate, by taking a step forward; no word was spoken by the candidate and no formal vow was involved. The order of service uses these words:

After you have received this Order, you will no more be free to change your mind; you will remain bound to the service of God, to serve whom is to reign. Aided by his grace, you will be bound to observe chastity and to be ministers of his Church forever. Therefore, while there is time, reflect. If you desire to persevere in your holy resolve, come forward in the name of the Lord.

The rubric, which immediately follows this prayer, says, 'The Ordinands advance one step'. 'Taking the step' bound the candidate to canon 132 (Old Code) of Canon Law.

The Ordination service was conducted completely in Latin and took anything up to three hours, according to the number of candidates for each of the Minor or Major Orders.

The prayers given below are, in each case, one of the principal prayers used prior to the 1970s in the conferring of a particular Order.

1959

9 June	Applications submitted for the Tonsure
10 July	Call to the Tonsure given
19 September	*After a retreat led by Father Laurence OFM*

Ordination: Tonsure conferred

The bishop prayed: 'Grant, we beseech thee, Almighty God, that these thy servants may forever persevere in thy love, for it is because of their love for thee that we have tonsured them today. And do thou keep them forever without stain. Amen.'

1960

3 March	Applications submitted for First Minor Orders
30 March	Call to First Minor Orders given
11 June	*After a retreat led by Father Bernard Bassett*

Ordination: First Minor Orders (Doorkeeper and Reader) conferred

The bishop prayed: 'Holy Lord, Father Almighty, vouchsafe to bless these thy servants for the office of Readers. May they by diligent practice of reading acquire knowledge and skill, say what is to be done, and carry out in their works what they say, so that by the example of holiness in word and deed they may promote the cause of Holy Church. Through Christ our Lord. Amen.'

1961

4 March	Applications submitted for Second Minor Orders
31 March	Call to Second Minor Orders given
27 May	*After a retreat led by Father Stephen OFM*

Ordination: Second Minor Orders (Exorcist and Acolyte) conferred

The bishop prayed: 'Dearly beloved brethren, let us humbly beseech God, the Father Almighty, to bless these his servants for the Order of Acolyte, that as they carry the material light in their hands, they may also send forth a spiritual light by their example, through the help of Our Lord Jesus Christ, and the Holy Ghost who liveth and reigneth, world without end. Amen.'

1962

16 March	Applications submitted for Subdiaconate
17 April	Call to the Subdiaconate given
4 June	All candidates swore the Anti-Modernist Oath
16 June	*After a retreat led by the Carmelite Prior of Aylesford, Fr Lynch*

Ordination: Subdiaconate conferred

The bishop prayed: 'Let us beseech our God and Lord to pour out his blessing upon these his servants, whom he has deigned to call to the office of Subdeacons. May they be faithful ministers in his sight and merit for themselves the reward laid up for the saints, by the help of our Lord Jesus Christ, who liveth and reigneth with him in the unity of the Holy Ghost, world without end. Amen.'

22 June	Applications submitted for the Diaconate
3 July	Call to the Diaconate given

| 22 September | *After a retreat led by Father Malachy, a Capuchin* |
| | **Ordination: Diaconate conferred** |

The bishop prayed: 'Hear, O Lord, our prayer and pour out upon these thy servants the Spirit who brings thy blessing, so that enriched with heavenly gifts they may be pleasing to thy majesty and give to their fellow men the example of a blameless life. Through our Lord Jesus Christ. Amen.'

1963

28 February	Applications submitted for the priesthood
9 April	Call to the priesthood given
8 June	*After a retreat led by Father Michael Hollings*
	Ordination: Priesthood conferred

The bishop prayed: 'Grant, we implore thee, Almighty Father, to these thy servants the dignity of the Priesthood, renew within them the spirit of holiness, that they may keep the rank in thy service which they have received from thee, and by their conduct may afford a pattern of holy living. Amen.'

The newly ordained priests were, after the service, conducted to a place where they could bestow a first blessing upon parents, family and friends. After lunch all depart for their home parishes and their first Mass the next day.

Ordination Prayer Card

Each newly ordained priest, by tradition, has an ordination card to give out to family, friends and parishioners, to mark the day and request prayers. Kevin Pelham's card, reproduced below, is typical of all the cards marking 8 June 1963.

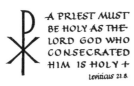

A PRIEST MUST BE HOLY AS THE LORD GOD WHO CONSECRATED HIM IS HOLY +

Leviticus 21.8.

Please Pray For

Kevin Michael Pelham

Ordained Priest at Wonersh

June 8th 1963

That he may be a holy priest.

Bless, O Lord, my parents and family and all who have + helped me to become your priest.

II
In the active ministry

Richard Quinlan

Canon Richard Quinlan is parish priest of Our Lady of Pity and St Simon Stock, Putney, South West London, in the archdiocese of Southwark

My family, who lived at Tullamore in the centre of Ireland for 20 years of my youth, were instrumental in my vocation. It happened very simply. One evening, when I was about 15, my parents said to me, 'What career do you have in mind; what do you want to be?' Up to that point I'd never thought much about it. For some unexplained reason, I replied, 'I think I'd like to be a priest.' My dad, who was a very practical sort of a man, said, 'We'll see!' About two months later he returned to the subject. 'Do you remember saying that you would like to be a priest? Are you still thinking about it?' 'Well, I haven't thought much about it since then,' I replied. 'We met a priest last night from the Liverpool diocese,' my dad went on. 'They have a junior seminary and are looking for young men in Ireland to work in England. Would you like to go to England to study? You can make up your mind as you go along.' 'I don't mind,' was my somewhat ambivalent reply.

The next thing that happened was that my uncle, Michael Quinlan, a priest in the Southwark Diocese, heard of this conversation and got in touch. 'If you are coming to England,' he said, 'come to Southwark. We have a junior seminary in Sussex, at St Joseph's, Mark Cross.'

It so happened that that year, 1954, my parents were planning to take their summer holiday in September at Bournemouth. It was arranged that I would accompany them. We had made application to Southwark and I needed to be interviewed. All the other candidates for Mark Cross had been interviewed in May or June. Archbishop Cowderoy interviewed me on 8 September. Straight afterwards he told his secretary to phone the Junior Seminary and tell them that I'd be coming down that very afternoon. My parents, who had accompanied me to the interview, took me down.

The Rector, Monsignor Corbishley (known affectionately to all as Corby) had lit a fire downstairs in the bishop's room and a beautiful table for tea had been set. Maurice Byrne, acting as the Rector's assistant, showed me around upstairs. What I didn't realise, until later, was that all the professors had been students with my uncle at the senior seminary. That was a terrific bonus, to start off like that. I had two years at Mark Cross, starting in the Year called 'Rudiments' and loved my time there. I wasn't keen on the long country walks, but I enjoyed the sports life there. As well as learning to play cricket there was plenty of football in the winter months.

It became obvious that I wasn't making academic progress because I was repeating a lot of things that I had already done at school in Ireland. It was decided that it would be a good idea if I went to Osterley (a college for late vocations in West London run by the Jesuits). Corby wrote to my parents, who were immediately concerned because they didn't know what Osterley was. They rang up to ask if anything was wrong, and, once they were reassured, I went to Osterley for one year before going on in 1957 to St John's, at Wonersh, rejoining those who were coming up from Mark Cross. I was happy at Wonersh. I enjoyed the old traditional game of Catte and times spent out jogging on the long days out to places like Box Hill. I enjoyed the routine, too, together with the peace and quiet, although I must say that towards the end of the six years I began to think that there was nothing to the priesthood but study, exams and holidays, repeated again and again. I've no criticism of the seminary training; I'm enormously appreciative of what Wonersh did for me. It opened my mind to see how the Church is continually challenging us to adapt to life as it unfolds. I was grateful also for the quality of the professors we had in our time; men like Edward Sillem, Dick Stewart and Charlie Wroe. They were wonderful people. The highlight of Wonersh, for me, was passing out of the Philosophy years into Theology, because I never understood Philosophy! I thought it was Geometry or something! I was more in touch with what the priesthood was about when I started Theology; the Philosophy years were like two years of a novitiate. Apart from the Philosophy, though, it was a good course and the tutors did a good job with us.

My first appointment, in 1963, was to Woolwich, with Canon Monk, who was 86 years of age when I was sent to him. The parish of Woolwich was terrific; unlike anything I've found since: a real community. You had people and families who had lived there for five or six generations. They had grown up together, living in the same roads, going to the same marketplace and the same church. We had everything going for us. There was the Army – the Royal Artillery – with the Army hospital, the Royal Herbert, and the Brook hospital. Then there was the maternity hospital to look after, and on the education side there was St Paul's Catholic secondary, at Plumstead, the private Notre Dame Convent school in Herbert Road and, of course, St Peter's, the parish primary school. The hospitals, particularly, kept us busy and it was quite possible to be called out, on a sick call, twice in the one night. I remember cycling up the hill to the Brook Hospital and the doctor meeting me for the second or third time; he wondered – as I did – if I ever went to bed! But you just took it in your stride; you were expected to be up next morning for Mass, with the daily routine following as usual.

After a while we developed the Youth Centre. The pressing need for provision for young people was obvious and we had the premises. I became enthusiastically involved, and happily it was a great success, ending up with 1200 members. We had two full-time leaders and about five part-time leaders, and, on top of that, a little group of volunteers. It was a great meeting place for the young people, where many made new friends.

Later, we converted the old school buildings, alongside the church, into a community centre. We were very pleased when the local Moslem community in Woolwich started using the building for regular meetings, like the month of Ramadan, or for a funeral.

In the Community Centre we set up a centre for free legal aid, a little nursery school, a group for battered wives and an old people's club. The Scouts, Cubs, Guides and Brownies also used the building, and we held lots of parish social activities there too. It was a very busy and exciting time.

Five of us occupied the priests' house: Canon Monk, Mick Gwinnell, Bill McBride, Joe Collins and myself. We all got on terrifically well. Material comforts were few: just one telephone between the five of us, one loo, and a bath that didn't work! The canon used to take himself off once a month down to the town hall and have his bath, for one shilling and six pence. In contrast to the comforts most of us enjoy today it was a sparse lifestyle – just the essentials – but there was a great spirit between us, not because of our situation but because of the work we were doing. After lunch together, we would all go into the church to say our prayers (for the conversion of England!) and then return for coffee around the table and chitchat. It was our main time together each day. The canon would smoke a cigar and halfway through would always fall asleep! We would take the cigar out of his fingers, put it in the ashtray, and quietly leave the room.

When I arrived in Woolwich, the Canon, at 86, was still going strong. He had been a curate there 50 years before, and had experienced a rough road to the priesthood. One of the first students at Wonersh, he had faced family opposition in studying there. At his ordination his father would not accept his blessing because he did not approve of him becoming a Catholic priest. Not only that, he disinherited him in his will. For four years he was my parish priest, providing a great example. Eventually, after a two-year illness, he died in 1970, aged 91. There are countless stories about 'the Canon'. On one of his annual visits to Lourdes (he was a Canon of Lourdes) he was filmed by the BBC in a railway carriage, talking to Malcolm Muggeridge about what it is to be a Catholic.

I had eleven and half happy years in Woolwich, the highlights of which were working with young people and helping to develop the community centre. Then, with all my books and bits and pieces, I moved to Balham, in Southwest London. I had never heard of the parish before and didn't know quite where it was. When I arrived I was told that my work during that day was to be in St James's hospital, as chaplain, and the rest of the time was to be for the parish. It was an interesting change. In Woolwich I had been accustomed to having a lot of responsibility; responsible for thousands of pounds going through the system while administering the £60,000 in grants that youth and community centres received, out of which I had salaries and so forth to pay. In Balham I didn't have responsibility for any money at all, not even for buying postage stamps! My job was in the hospital, and, of course, saying the morning Mass in the parish. At first I found this lack of responsibility strange and disturbing.

At the hospital I started visiting and getting to know people; working, particularly, with the Anglican chaplain, Henry Theobald. One day, at the bedside of a patient, I was telling him about the community centre at Woolwich and my youth work. 'Listen,' he suddenly said, 'I'm in hospital. Tell me about God!' And I got hopelessly stuck; completely inarticulate! I didn't want to come out with platitudes but I didn't want to put the man off. Suddenly, and unexpectedly, I was face to face with myself. What am I? Was I ordained to be a youth worker or community worker, or was the priesthood the first thing in my life? That man's question stopped me in my tracks. It made me think deeply about what my priesthood was about. It was the first time that I had been seriously challenged about it. That led in turn to questions about my spiritual life. It was a truly life-changing experience. Looking back, I could see what had happened. I'd been ordained, full of enthusiasm, but there hadn't been a lot to do in the parish, so I'd got involved with the youth club, which led on to the development of the community centre. This all meant that I wasn't developing the priestly qualities that I should have been developing. Reflection on my spiritual life encouraged me to take up the opportunity of a sabbatical in 1977 for six months.

I went to Rome and stayed in a house where there were priests and deacons from around the world. It was six months of formation, on the theme 'Being the priest the Church needs today'. It was a wonderful experience, like being pared down to your bones and new flesh being put on again. I didn't actually learn anything new, but I was hearing it afresh, in a different challenging setting.

I returned reinvigorated to Balham and changed from being a curate who was used to doing his own thing to being a curate working in collaboration with the parish priest. In the first year I felt that the parish priest was a little Hitler, but in fact I was still stuck in my own individualistic way of looking at things and working. Once I came to look at parochial life as a whole, I began to see things through the eyes of the parish priest, and I changed. So, after I'd done my hospital work, I went visiting; there was nothing else to do. The parish priest looked after everything that happened inside the house; the books, the baptisms, the marriages and so forth, so I set out to visit everyone in the parish and made a register. Before I went out, I would inform the parish priest of those I hoped to see and on my return I would update him on those I had actually seen. He always briefed me before I went and it was good for him to be filled in afterwards. Parishioners would say, 'Why are *you* visiting, and not the parish priest?' 'He sent me,' I would answer. 'I'm here in his name.'

We acquired premises in the Balham parish, near Clapham College, and set up a little social club. Knowing I'd had the experience of the club in Woolwich, the parish priest said to me, 'There is the cheque book; spend what you like! But do it right.' We formed a committee of great people, both men and women, who set up the club on a sure foundation. We called it the Oliver Plunkett Club, and it still exists.

Another highlight in Balham for me was the third centenary of the marytrdom of St Oliver Plunkett, in July 1981. One of our chapels-of-ease in the parish was dedicated to him, but the principal reason for my interest was that Martin Bennett, the parish priest, had a special devotion to St Oliver and had written a book about him. We arranged for the saint's body to be brought back from Downside and invited Cardinal Tomas O' Fiaich from Ireland and Lord Norfolk to be involved, organising a great celebration on Clapham Common with thousands of people present, including many bishops from the UK and abroad. At the end of the Mass the Abbot of Downside took the body of St Oliver back to Downside Abbey. The planning took about four years and cost a fortune, but it was all paid for by generous donations.

My appointment as parish priest, in 1981, was to Putney; obviously the archbishop was inspired when he made the appointment! Joe Kelly, the previous parish priest (who had been in Putney for 28 years) was still in the parish house, but partly retired. He did not enjoy good health. When he retired fully, in an apartment in the parish, it was time for the laity to be involved. For me that was easy, given the experiences I'd had. It was imperative for the laity to share in the ministry of the Church. The great thing I soon discovered about the parish is that it is blessed with people with enormous ability and wonderfully generous with their time. We have many church structures – for catechising, the confirmation programme, First Communion, Sunday school, eucharistic ministers, finance committee, Justice and Peace group, choir and so on – and I see my role as being the one who affirms them and attempts to involve new members of the parish to share in our life.

About 11 years ago the Westminister and Southwark dioceses started a Programme called 'Education for Parish Service' (EPS). It was a course to empower the laity for pastoral ministry. Started by Cardinal Basil Hume and Archbishop Michael Bowen, it was centred on Allan Hall in Chelsea, but more recently it has moved across the Thames to the Southwark Christian Education Centre. I'm a trustee of that, as well as chaplain to the students. The course consists of two years' formation for laity to take on leadership roles. We've had two or three people from our parish going on to the programme each year. It gives them confidence about their faith and a sense of permanence in ministry. They can face crises and not give up when the going gets tough. All those people are now on our parish team, which meets every Monday. There we discuss what we are doing pastorally from week to week in the parish. I have various pastoral assistants, who each receive a salary from the parish. Our parish secretary is also paid, and we have a permanent deacon here, who is an invaluable help.

I've noticed and tried to cultivate a shift in myself from being an individual-minded parish priest to becoming more communitarian. That's not just a technique taken from the business world and the city; rather it's more of a spiritual and theological way of working; a Gospel and early-Church approach towards ministry. What do I mean by that? To be honest, I'm still working on the idea. It's certainly a more trinitarian view of ministry, imitating the relationships we find in the Trinity. Somehow in all of us involved in pastoral ministry there needs to be a dying and rising again, a dying to 'my' ideas and a rising to the ideas and inspirations that come from others. So collaboration in the parish setting means emptying oneself of the 'old man' and one's own way of doing things. It's a difficult process to go through; no one should imagine it's easy. We are very possessive of our own ideas; I see collaborative ministry as all about trying to let them go and encouraging others to grow. Parish priests of the future need to be facilitators, making it possible for people to live the gospel. The buzzword for this is 'empowering' people.

I welcomed the changes made by the Second Vatican Council, personally having no problems with any of them. I remember an *Ad Clerum* coming from Archbishop Cyril Cowderoy saying that if you wanted to read your breviary in English you had to apply to him for permission. I applied, and permission was granted, signed by Cyril, but it was given to me in Latin! 'What a twist!' I thought. All the reforms and changes made sense to me. As time went on I warmed to them still more, but we are still assimilating the full implications of Vatican II and will be for the next 60 years. The Church has become less hierarchical and more community-based, but we are constantly learning how to live in community.

The liturgical reforms of Vatican II were liberating; it was delightful to be able to read the Gospel directly to the people in their own language. It was a nonsense to read it in Latin first, then go up in the pulpit and read it to them again in English.

What has consistently given me real joy is seeing people working together. In the Youth Centre, in Woolwich, that was in the form of a committee; 24 of us around a table. There would be 12 from the management team and 12 young people sitting side by side around the table, each trying to reach a consensus on a way of working. I enjoyed working with that arrangement. Here, at Putney, we have teams for everything: five couples help with the engaged couples programme (60-80 couples a year take the course). There are six couples on the team for the baptismal programme. I also enjoy working with the large team that prepares the children for First Holy Communion. When I stop and ask myself what I have achieved, my answer is that I enjoy getting people to work together; seeing them comfortable with each other and, hopefully, competent. That gives me great pleasure.

On the other hand, my darkest hour was that day already referred to in the hospital, when the patient there said to me, 'Tell me about God', and I couldn't. Knowing that I couldn't pull the wool over his eyes forced me back to the drawing board, making me ask myself, 'What have I become?' Sadly I can see other priests making the same mistake I made; young fellows coming out with great enthusiasm, getting involved in all sorts of non-priestly activities. There's a constant danger that such activities will take you away from your prime purpose. Although I really enjoyed the work of the Woolwich Centre, it unquestionably drained me of spirituality. Another thing that hurts is when people you trust, having nurtured and built them up, just throw it aside and give up. It is so disappointing when you put a lot of store in a person and their ministry to see them turn their back on it and walk away. That's why I think the formation we give people, educating them for parish service (EPS) is a God-send. It gives them a way of thinking that puts charity first. They learn that the Church is a sacrament of love and forgiveness. When we start judging one another and evaluating one another, as if we were in some city office, then we are falling through the floor.

I haven't thought much about the way students for the priesthood should be trained in the future. I do feel though that there should be more of a balance between the formation given in the seminary – important as it is – and the time spent in parishes. I understand that seminaries are doing more of this now, as distinct from our day. If I were to give any advice to a young man about to be ordained, I'd say, 'Never leave your wallet in your jacket-pocket in the sacristy while you're celebrating Mass'! Seriously, though, it's hard to give people advice. I don't think that I would presume to give any; I'd look for ways of affirming them and their goodness, and leave it at that. What I *would* do however is encourage any priest that expressed interest to go on a sabbatical, ongoing formation course or specialised training of some kind. If I were bishop, I'd be encouraging – and paying for – all my priests to go on such courses. At present, sadly, it's the same few priests that go all the time. Every priest has a talent or gift to be discovered and nurtured.

Looking back over the years, one of the most valuable things that the seminary gave me was a little question mark. It made me realise that I don't know much and instilled sufficient curiosity inside me to inspire a bit of regular reading and attendance at study days and such like. One more recent turning point for me was when, a few years ago, I was invited to lead a novena of prayer – a novena of grace for Ireland – in an Irish parish. Now with my background and history you would have thought I'd know that 'novena' means nine but somehow I'd got the idea in my head that 'novena' meant three! So I accepted, thinking I was to give three talks and speak at two Masses on 'What is a parish?' only to discover, to my astonishment, when I went to the Irish parish for interview six months beforehand, that I had to talk for nine days! Three priests there were new to the parish and wanted to start off their ministries with a common, shared vision, carrying their people with them. It took me six months to put my little homilies together – and three months to recover afterwards! It was so draining. The point of the story is what it did for me. It helped me to gain a vision of what a parish should be. That was a real high point for me and has led me to reproduce the material in a little handbook, recently published by Kevin Mayhew, titled *A Community Afire!* Its theme is not 'what is a parish?' but 'how do we live being a parish?' Based upon the theology and spirituality of communion and collaboration it is my hope that it will be of value to students participating in the Education for Parish Service programme, both here at Tooting, and elsewhere.

Anthony Shelley

Father Tony Shelley is parish priest of St Wilfrid's, Hailsham, East Sussex, in the Diocese of Arundel and Brighton

I was born in December 1937 in Ewell, Surrey and, while still too young to remember, the family moved to Brighton – to give London a wide berth during the War. I was the oldest of three, with a sister and a brother. Our family life was very caring, with a firm discipline, but not in any way overbearing. My father was a Catholic, as was my mother, who is now in nursing care. We never questioned our Catholic upbringing and regularly walked to church Sunday by Sunday.

As soon as I was old enough I was keen to be an altar server, partly due – I think – to my admiration and liking of the priests in the Parish of St Mary's, Preston Park. From my early years I thought I would like to be a priest. I continued being an altar server, despite the stewardship of a parish priest who frequently declared that he 'hated boys' and who would throw us off the sanctuary for the slightest misdemeanour. I think he had his reasons! On one occasion, after parking his 'Mini' facing forwards, before Mass, he came out of the church to find it facing the other direction! On another occasion, whilst he was hearing Confessions, the electricity was switched off and, much to the surprise of the dear lady in the confessional, a great roar came from the confessional box bringing down curses on boys everywhere! I cannot remember exactly how I came to be around on these occasions!

Before going to the Xaverian College, Brighton, I was sent to Lourdes Convent, Brighton; a girls' school where boys were accepted for the junior years only. It was an extremely rigid French convent school, where the girls had to curtsey should Reverend Mother pass by. She expelled me for a week, for allegedly calling an old lady a witch (in fact I was saying rather loudly to my friend that I thought she *looked* like a witch). Thinking I would have a nice week off, I was well and truly gated by my mother.

Another early influence on the development of my vocation occurred when I was about ten. My Dad took me to the Carthusian monastery at Parkminister, near West Grinstead in Sussex. The monks wanted to listen to the recording of the Gelineau psalms, but the voltage in the monastery was too low for them to use a standard record player. My father went there to sort it out. One of the monks gave me a book of prayers, which I treasured for many years. That little book meant a lot to me and was influential with regard to my subsequent development.

Then I went to senior school, the Xaverian College at Brighton. While there, in my early teens, the idea of the priesthood drifted away, but towards the end of my time with the Xaverians, it came back – I was inspired by other lads from the same school. There were quite a lot of us there considering the priesthood. I particularly remember Kevin Gaskin, who went off to the seminary. That resurrected and stirred the idea in me. David Weston joined us later.

In my ordination Year there were three old-Xaverians: Michael Ivers and Ken Bell from Clapham College, and Stephen Hinde from Mayfield College.

In 1954 I was sent to Mark Cross for three years. I accepted the boarding-school life for what it was; it wasn't awful, but you always pined for the holidays! You lived in a little bit of fear, as you had to live by 'the Rule'. I could never have managed six years, although I wasn't unduly unhappy at Mark Cross; it was my desire to be a priest that kept me going.

On arrival at Wonersh in 1957 I thought the seminary training was fine, though looking back now I wouldn't agree that it was the most appropriate training. I found it quite tough, but, as at Mark Cross, my determination to be ordained kept me going. I still vividly recall, to this day, a part of the daily lunchtime reading (we had a book read to us while we ate our midday meal) that must have bypassed the censor. The passage described a seminary as 'an institution, which is a cross between a kindergarten and an army barracks'. I remember that the silence ended and brought the house down!

I also remember nearly being thrown out of Mark Cross – at least, I thought, at the time I was going to be sent home. It happened because I wanted to listen to some opera (an interest at that time) on the radio and I went to Corby (Monsignor Ernest Corbishley, Rector of the seminary) to ask for his permission to listen to the programme. He was shocked beyond words! He indignantly refused and I really thought he was going to throw me out. That reminds me of the time, just before we became sub-deacons, when we all went to the theatre and the opera for what we thought would be the last time. In those years the Theatre Law (Westminster Council of 1873) was in force, which forbade clerics in major Orders from attending the theatre (even for Shakespeare, the opera or ballet) under pain of mortal sin and automatic excommunication! So, as was the custom, we all went off to see what plays and shows we could see before it was too late. I went to see a musical with Stephen Hinde, others went to the Old Vic to watch Shakespeare and some to Covent Garden to enjoy *Aida*.

Looking back I can say that the training was too monastic; we were not going to be living with monks after ordination! It was as if the Church had not developed a spirituality and preparation for life in the world. Naturally, at the time, we accepted Wonersh training just as it was and I suppose it did prepare us for how the Church was then. In those days priests were placed on pedestals and people almost bowed and cowered in their presence. Emphasis was placed on little things, like the dressing-up in the uniform of cassocks and birettas, which we wore all day, every day, in the seminary. Looking back, I now view it quite differently. It was a training far removed from being an adequate preparation for real life out in a parish. Surprisingly, for example, we were never taught to pray.

Perhaps reflecting this lack of formal training in prayer, at various points of my life I looked for ways of deepening my prayer-life, using certain experiences as a means to develop my seeking after God. One or two retreats stand out particularly in my mind; for example the 40-day retreat at St Buenos and silent retreats at

Taizé. To see a thousand young people or more reaching out to God in prayer, as at Taizé, is a very powerful and sometimes humbling experience; it has certainly helped me to develop my spiritual life. Another valuable imprint upon me was my regular pilgrimages to Lourdes with sixth-formers and sick and disabled pilgrims; an imprint that I shall always treasure.

I was a long time – five or six years I think – in my first appointment at St Leonards-on-Sea, Sussex. There were three curates, all newly ordained, and Ed O'Shea, the parish priest. He'd just come from teaching at the St John Fisher School and he was a man of his time, although not too traditional. A period of working on the missions made quite an impact on him, and all who had the good fortune to work with him. In St Leonards the three curates teamed up, which proved a real support and helped us along.

A considerable amount of youth work came my way and I instigated a number of projects. There were some wonderfully crazy things, like a relay run from St Leonards on the Sussex coast to Tony Castle's youth group at Nunhead, Peckham, in South London. I even ran a part of the 60-plus miles. St Leonards was a great learning experience; I assimilated a great deal in that parish, especially from working with the local youth authorities. I've remained in youth work in all sorts of ways over the years. Hospitals, schools and caring for the elderly were also part of my first appointment, giving me a broad band of experience.

While I was there, the Diocese of Southwark was split into two parts; the new Diocese of Arundel and Brighton coming into existence. The change was real cloak and dagger stuff! Andrew Beer, the deanery secretary to Tom Lynch, rang me up one day and said, 'As from midday today you are in the Diocese of Arundel and Brighton'! It was all done secretly; no one knew beforehand, no one was consulted.

Michael Bowen, who had just become the new auxiliary bishop, visited the parish and said to me 'What are you doing here? You were suppose to have moved!' So I waited and waited for a wretched letter to turn up telling me where to go. When it eventually arrived I was sent, for a short stint to Reigate, to look after the parish priest, Gerry O'Sullivan, who was a nervous, ill man. As a result of the Second Vatican Council, everything was changing – and he couldn't handle any change. Having come from a parish where I'd been hospital chaplain, school and convent chaplain, I found there was absolutely nothing like that at Reigate. It was a lonely, hard appointment. Angela Lawrence, later well known in Diocesan circles, lived in the parish. She gave me a hand to put some modern thoughts before Gerry O'Sullivan, but the poor man couldn't cope with them! I think he was glad to get rid of me! Pretty quickly I was moved on from there to Crawley.

I went there as curate to Ken McCarthy, and lived at Langley Green with him until I went to the Broadfield estate and moved into a semi-detached house. An Anglican priest, a URC minister and I were given a plot of land, and told by our separate Church authorities to get together and build three churches with a communal area between us; an ecumenical car park! Happily, we eventually persuaded them to grant us permission to build one shared church and then, later, to allow the local authorities to build a community centre within the church complex, although it took the local authorities quite a while to overcome their suspicions concerning our intentions before agreeing.

While there I began helping out at St Wilfrid's Catholic Comprehensive School, Crawley as Chaplain – taking the place of a Franciscan priest; an experience I found quite daunting. During that period I started the Sixth-form Pilgrimage to Lourdes, which has been going every year for the last 35 years. I obtained a licence to drive one of the Across Trust's jumblances (a converted coach, equipped with beds to transport sick pilgrims), as a voluntary driver. First we had one jumblance-load, then a jumblance and minibus. We ran those pilgrimages annually for many years, several times having to endure the 'Gestapo' in Lourdes; that is, the over-officious guardians of the Shrine. On one occasion we went to make the torchlight procession in the pouring rain. We were accompanying dying pilgrims who would not live to see the official Lourdes season. A priest came over and said, 'You can't do this.' We stood there, the rain pouring down on our sick and invalid pilgrims, and I thought to myself what a 'lovely' image of the Church this was for these sixth-form helpers. I had a French-trained priest with me who told the official, 'Your attitude, and your keeping the dying and sick waiting in the pouring rain, will be in the local paper tomorrow.' The official relented and we were allowed to join the procession, on condition that we walked in silence and did not join in saying the Rosary out loud! I was in at the beginning of the Across Trust, with their jumblances, one of the volunteer drivers who helped to get the scheme off the ground. Then they started paying professional drivers and our services were dispensed with.

After Crawley I went to the Maryvale Pastoral Centre at Bramley, near Guildford, for a couple of years. The Franciscan Missionaries of the Divine Motherhood (FMDM) nuns were still there running things and my role wasn't very clear, so at times things got a little difficult. Anyway, I spent two years there, and it proved to be a good experience. The Centre had been a House of Prayer, but had gradually become a little more youth orientated. I found it a strange experience, welcoming and befriending all those who came only to be saying goodbye to them within a couple of days, with little expectation of seeing them again. Actually, quite a number of young people came back under their own steam to do odd jobs and help out around the house. Several kept in touch and made a genuine effort to develop their faith through discussions and the Sacrament of Reconciliation. While I was at Maryvale, because the priest was ill, I also ran the adjoining Bramley Parish.

From Maryvale I went as parish priest to Worthing, which was where Monsignor Iggleden, who had been the Rector in our days at Wonersh, had been parish priest. The bishop, Cormac Murphy O'Connor (now Cardinal), had told me to reorder the church for the new liturgy. At the biggest parish meeting I've ever seen, I was surprised by the way the people, largely elderly folk, accepted the reordering plans. I realise now, looking back, that I didn't always use the right language when explaining what I had in mind.

For example, we didn't use all new modern materials, instead reusing existing material in new places and new ways. There was a little opposition. My biggest critic and opposer, once she saw what we had done, was impressed and gave me a substantial cheque towards the costs.

While I was at Worthing, the Diocese of Arundel and Brighton conducted the process called 'Renew' which aimed to apply the teaching of the Second Vatican Council to the renewal of the diocese. It was a good scheme, and in my opinion it went well. I was always enthusiastic about anything that applied or furthered the teaching of the Council.

I'd been at Worthing for five or six years when I contracted an unusual viral infection – I felt absolutely deflated and, more worrying, depressed. I'd never been depressed in my life before. So I went to the doctor. 'Oh,' he said, 'a bug is going around. What you need is rest.' My parents were in Hong Kong visiting my brother at the time, so I decided to go home, shut myself off and rest. It wasn't long enough.

When the bishop asked me to consider going to Epsom, he gave me plenty of warning and told me to seek advice first. I thought that I was perhaps getting a bit stale and in need of a change, so I accepted the appointment; but Epsom, brimful of hospitals, is a tough nut. After a year and a half I just crashed out! The bishop visited and told me that he was worried about me. I replied that I was barely holding myself together, having no energy or enthusiasm for anything. Anyway, to cut a long story short, I was taken off duty; at that time the diocese was not well equipped to care with such situations. For four years I was placed on the wrong medication, so naturally there was very little progress or improvement. I didn't know what was wrong with me and no one else seemed to have any idea either. The illness seemed to bring on stress; I wanted to be active but couldn't be. I started to wonder about all sorts of things. Am I losing my faith? Am I fed up with the priesthood? Everything was going through my mind.

After a long break I began to feel a bit better, but the bishop said that I was not to return to Epsom. The Director of St Buenos,

Damien Jackson – who I met when he visited his sister, who happened to live in the parish – invited me to St Buenos. I went down there for a 40-day retreat, which Damien adapted for my needs. It was a great and valuable experience.

Apparently recovered, I was appointed to Shoreham-on-Sea, to take over from John Medcalf, who was off to Latin America. After a couple of years I crashed out there! I rested up at Redhill for a bit and had some therapy. I was then appointed to Burgess Hill and came across a priest in the diocese who had not been well either. He was seeing an Indian doctor, not a Christian, who had helped him. I met this doctor, told him my story and he listened to everything I had to say. He was very holistic and immediately changed the medication. Meanwhile more and more priests within the diocese were finding themselves in need of help. On one occasion when I went to see this doctor, he told me that he was spending the whole weekend seeing priests from all over the country.

One day the bishop called me up and asked me to go temporarily to Hailsham – where I am now. I told him that I would move, but would prefer a permanent appointment; so I have been here, happily and in good health, for the last three years.

I've always been eager for the Church to move on and, since the Second Vatican Council, I've been comfortable working with anything new. I can still see enormous gaps, various things crying out loud at me. The Church, sadly, is out of touch and has a poor image. I don't just mean because of child abuse and that sort of thing. I mean, equally, such things as the number of priests ordained who are 'ultra-conservatives'. I've been told that many of those who offer themselves for the priesthood are turned down because of their extreme views. You have to ask, what sort of image of 'Church' are we projecting? Looking back over the years I've always valued my contact with young people, which I believe has invariably been good. On the negative side, people who are entrenched, narrow and reactionary have got under my skin!

Over the years much has changed in the Church for the better, but there is still some way to go. Relations between clergy and laity have moved some way from 'them and us'. In these challenging times for the Church both priests and people need to discern their roles much more clearly; it will require a lot of 'letting go' and 'taking on board'. The liturgy is improving but still smacks of a monastic tradition, which is alien to life in today's world.

Another very simple thing: why are so many churches still draughty, cold, uncomfortable, poorly lit and without adequate audio provision? If we really value what it is we experience in the community of the Church, why do we not show it in the way we enhance our places of worship? If we went to a concert hall, a theatre or a restaurant that was drab and uncomfortable, we would, more than likely, not go there again. Simple things like this can make all the difference – and indeed already have, where they have been implemented.

A candidate for the priesthood today needs to have a strong and uncomplicated faith based on personal prayer, with a wholesome experience of what it is to live in today's world; and be ready to help those who live in that world. It concerns me that there seems to be what I would call a 'right wing' element amongst some younger clergy. Their approach can be unbalanced, more interested in preserving the truth of the faith and worship of the past than in communicating it in a way that can be appreciated and lived in the present. It is very challenging to offer oneself for the priesthood today, and I feel personally that seminaries are still finding their way.

I have always found departures and farewells difficult, so it was with sadness that I learnt of some members of my Year leaving the priesthood relatively early on after ordination. In some cases I know that there were particular circumstances underlying their decisions that the Church cannot be proud of, but all of us are human and sometimes our timing can be bad. Our generation still had the notion that anyone who left the seminary – let alone the priesthood – was a failure and a disgrace to his family and the Church.

As the years have passed death has taken its toll: Ken Snaith and, prematurely, Stephen Hinde. At the time I thought, this can't be happening to my Year; ordination seemed to be only a few years away. It was the sudden and unexpected death of John Medcalf that forcefully brought home the realisation that although we share in the eternal priesthood of Christ, we ourselves don't yet share eternity here!

The two of our number (Ken Bell and Joe Ware) who were victims of serious road accidents (and miraculously survived) have become an inspiration and example to us all in so many ways. They cannot tell their stories as we can, but Joe (who I see regularly) is truly a priest in every sense of the word, every day. Ken I shall always remember for a very moving homily on 'suffering', which he shared at one of our class reunions. They have both been 'active' in their ministry in their own unique way, and it is my hope and prayer that their example might inspire others to a life of committed service in turn.

Kevin Pelham

Father Kevin Pelham is the parish priest of
St Margaret's, Carshalton Beeches, Surrey

I was born in North Cheam in 1938, one of the last generation of prewar babies, and one of the Second World War's first home-front victims as the family house fell to Hitler's blitz in 1940. Indeed my very earliest surviving memory – admittedly dim – was of being in an air-raid shelter. Thank God, though, none of us, – parents, elder brother Patrick or I – were in the house at the time. For the next nine years, we relied first on the hospitality of friends, then lived in an upstairs flat in the home of the local estate agent, and then rented for three and a half years a house we miraculously found unoccupied in an adjoining street. This too lost its ceilings and several windows when a doodlebug destroyed four houses just round the corner. Within the hour, Father Michael Quinlan, one of our parish curates (and now a retired Canon of the Arundel and Brighton Diocese) came round to make sure we were all right. It seems that parish visiting could be life threatening in those days.

After the war came two dire years in an asbestos-roofed Nissen Hut, where in winter (by which I mean that ghastly winter of 1947) you could write your name in the damp on the concrete floor. It was like heaven to be awarded the luxury of a prefab, where we lived until our original house was finally rebuilt in 1949. At last, I thought, some permanence; here we are back to stay. But no! What had been adequate for a family with a toddler and a baby seemed cramped with a couple of teenagers, so three years later we were on the move again. This time, though, my parents did put down roots, staying in the same house almost up to the time of their retirement, when they relocated to the South Coast.

My mother, Tipperary bred and born, was the 'original' Catholic. She had come over from Ireland in 1924. My father was received into the Church just a few weeks before they married – something I always advise engaged couples *against* doing. But in his case, his conversion was sincere and permanent, and right up until the end of his life he remained a committed and faithful Catholic. My brother migrated to Australia in 1965, where he and his wife raised three children and now have seven grandchildren. They make occasional visits back to the UK, and I have been six times to Australia, so we still see each other fairly often.

All the moves I detailed above were in the Cheam and North Cheam areas so, naturally, I attended Saint Cecilia's primary school. I think it was in the top infants' class there that I first remember being asked what I wanted to be when I grew up and even then replied, 'a priest'. How seriously I meant it at the time I really don't know. Scraping through the eleven-plus, I went on to Wimbledon College, run by the Jesuits. Since being ordained I have heard so many horror stories about schools and colleges run by religious, but that wasn't my experience. For the 1950s I found the Jesuits well ahead of their time; open and, for the most part, broad-minded. They were always ready to answer questions, never fobbing off an awkward religious query with a 'don't you dare question the Church's authority' type of answer. In all honesty, it was a happy time of my life; I had good friends in my class who took care of me (not only was I the smallest boy in the school when I started – to my chagrin and humiliation I remained the smallest boy for two years!); I had teachers who, for the most part (there was always the rare exception) were dedicated, and I had not too much trouble keeping up with the curriculum. Although (maybe because) I had no sporting skills, they gave me the job of Cricket Secretary in my final two years and entrusted me with arranging the inter-school fixtures for all the XIs.

After A-Levels, wanting to be a priest, I offered myself to the Southwark diocese and was interviewed by Bishop (as he then was) Cyril Cowderoy. Concerned that my Latin might have become rusty, as I had dropped it after O-Level, he sent me for one year, although I was 18, to the Junior Seminary at Mark

Cross. Life was strangely different at first. Once I had got to grips with some rather petty rules – like not going up or down stairs more than one at a time and not being allowed even to use a fountain pen – I settled in and despite the task of doing A-Level Latin in a single year, I still found the time to develop some Thespian traits, playing Molière's *Malade imaginaire* as well as the sister of an amateur-detective bishop in a now long-forgotten comedy thriller. I had a memorable final month at Mark Cross: after the A-levels had finished, while the rest of the College were still doing their 'O's and end-of-year exams, four of us had a great time re-painting the chicken runs on the poultry farm attached to the College – and the weather was delightful! It was a happy, pleasing way to end that period.

We were treated as adults at Wonersh – though a post-1950s generation might dispute that. With hindsight, I suppose it is possible to say how much better the education and conditions could have been, but in fairness one could not have expected the same type of existence – or freedoms – at a pre-Vatican Two Seminary as one would take for granted nowadays. It was, unashamedly, a closed community. But at the same time it was a community that gave scope for all kinds of interests, sports and activities. There were just so many things – nothing to do with the studies – to learn, do or develop an interest in, which I would never have had an opportunity to pick up elsewhere. For example, I learnt bookbinding, which from time to time still stands me in good stead – St Margaret's Altar Missal goes right back to the 1973 edition, but you'd never suspect that from the binding! There were all manner of house activities. One that sticks in my mind was the manufacture of Christmas decorations. The imagination and ingenuity that went into their preparation was amazing. Every year something absolutely novel was thought out. No boring paper streamers bought in the local shop, but themes and artwork specially designed and attractively displayed. Christmas, for me, was a joyous time. Yes, I know we should really have been with our families, but I never missed that because the community Christmas at Wonersh was so good.

Another area was sport. I'd been asthmatic as a young child and, other than cricket, never took part in sports at all. I outgrew the asthma at Wonersh and took up rugby, football, tennis, handball and catte. I was never any good at any of them, but at least I had the opportunity to get involved. Then, just like at Mark Cross, there was drama too. I was in all the Gilbert and Sullivan productions – for some reason always playing female roles: one of the Three Little Maids in *The Mikado*; Cousin Hebe in *H.M.S. Pinafore*, Ruth in *The Pirates of Penzance* and Dame Hannah in *Ruddigore*. I also enjoyed the experience in my fifth year of producing and directing a play, which gave me a great deal of confidence. Wonersh was very much a community and we simply had to get on with one another, in particular those with whom we were placed – for example, in the Refectory at mealtimes (the seating plan was changed three times each year). Most people managed to display the charity towards others that they were going to preach later. Seminaries have changed since then, mostly – but not always – for the better. One seminary I visited some years ago seemed to have no student community life at all (it now has a new Rector and things have improved). In my view, the process of building relationships within a diverse community is an obvious means of preparing students for the varied relationships they will need to forge with their parishioners after ordination.

Although I have no formal degree (BA Open University: failed!) I have, selectively, kept up with reading and study. I say 'selectively', because I make no excuse for having concentrated on topics that interest me: principally music and liturgy. Most years, recently, I have attended a liturgical or musical course and I am a member of the Panel of Monastic Musicians. Not that I'm in a monastery or have incredible musical skills; just that I have a love of music and of the many ways it can be used in the reformed liturgy. Thinking of the liturgy prompts me to say that I don't believe we were really taught how to pray in the seminary. The Rector talked about prayer from time to time, and we had a monthly half-day of recollection when an outside spiritual

Programme Cover

produced by Stephen Hinde
cover design by David Weston
(six of the Year were involved in this production)

director (always the same one) came and gave us a couple of conferences, but we were still left very much on our own. Maybe a different priest each month might have proved more fruitful – I believe they started doing that after I was ordained. I also found the half-hour meditation first thing in the morning at Wonersh, when I was still half- (maybe even three-quarters-) asleep, somewhat barren.

My ordination to the priesthood was during a papal interregnum. John XXIII had died just five days earlier. I won't say being ordained was the best day of my life – I'm convinced that day is still to come – let's just say it was the best so far! My first appointment was to St Joseph's, Roehampton, a parish that was being vacated by the Jesuits. So I didn't come into an existing set-up; the parish priest, together with Mike Ivers and I – both newly ordained curates – all started together. Mike and I were the two youngest to be ordained from Wonersh that year – the two most junior priests in the whole diocese – but he was four months younger than I was so I had the unique experience of starting off as a senior curate! My comeuppance came two years later when Michael was made assistant director to the Southwark Children's Society. The priest who took his place, Ronan Magner, was four years senior to me, so I was duly demoted.

From the beginning I got on well with Father (now Monsignor) Paddy Daly the parish priest. He had a 'spark' in him and a tremendous sense of humour. He had a few foibles I had to live with, but that would be true of anybody. Paddy was a great socialiser and very popular, and had had a very wide experience. After a few years as a schools' inspector, he'd been invited to join the Church's Diplomatic Service and had worked as private secretary to Archbishop Knox, the Apostolic Delegate to Kenya, whom he'd later followed to India where the archbishop became Papal Internuncio. It was a sad day when he left Roehampton to become Rector of Wonersh, just three weeks after Mike Ivers went to the Children's Society. The housekeeper – who admittedly had always said she would 'only do the job for Father Daly' – left at the same time, and even the supply priest who always said the

Sunday Evening Mass for us was called back by his bishop to his own country. As a result it felt as if I were the one who had been moved; it was a complete change for me.

When I began parish ministry I thought I was well prepared, and that, perhaps, proved a problem. A newly ordained priest can come out of the seminary thinking that he knows everything. In fact – as I'm prepared to admit 40 years on – I was totally inexperienced and let myself be drawn into several confrontations that even a modicum of maturity would have taught me how to avoid or sidestep.

The new parish priest, Father Hubert Simes, who took over the Roehampton parish from Father Daly, was a very different sort of man. He introduced a weekly 'business' meeting for the three of us – even though we saw one another at each meal – and immediately informed us, at the very first one, that our custom of each curate staying at home overnight after our day off – which Father Daly had encouraged in the interest of family closeness – was, according to canon law, legally dubious. At our second meeting we were told that the practice was to terminate the following week and that henceforth the 11 o'clock rule (all clergy to be back in the presbytery by that time) should be observed. And after that he never held another business meeting again! Although Father Simes was a very prayerful and, in his own way, a kind man, he always thought that if people took time, and prayed about a certain matter, they would come into agreement with him. He hated the idea of exercising his authority as a parish priest. Instead he wanted everyone to accept that whatever he was asking was the best – even the only – solution. He truly found it difficult to understand how people might in all sincerity disagree with him!

One thing I did learn from Father Simes and which I introduced here at Carshalton Beeches when I first became parish priest, was to have the weekly newsletter distributed to everyone, not just to those who pick it up on a Sunday at Mass. The whole parish is divided into about 34 areas of between 8 and 20 families. A team of four key-distributors deliver bulk copies to each of the local deliverers, so that every known Catholic in the parish, practising, non-practising or attending elsewhere, can receive the weekly newsletter. I've no doubt many copies go straight into the bin unread, but I'm equally sure it also keeps many others in touch, who otherwise would not be.

After four years in Roehampton, I received a new appointment. I can still remember Monsignor Gibney's (the vicar-general's) letter, word for word: 'Dear Father Pelham, the Archbishop has asked me to inform you that he has appointed you as assistant to Father Gleeson at Rainham. Kindly make arrangements with him when you go there. Yours sincerely, H Gibney VG.' So just ten days later, I had wound up all my Roehampton affairs and moved into St Thomas's parish at Rainham, near Gillingham, this time as neither junior nor senior but the *only* curate. Father John Gleeson was different again; he was from the West of Ireland and it was as though he'd never left there! At least I knew from the start where I was with him; he laid down the law in a fashion that Father Simes had always been reluctant to do. But he was impartial, laying down the law not just to me but also to the housekeeper, the servers, the school, the lay people, the Catholic Women's League, the voluntary parish helpers – everyone. Father Gleeson got through quite a number of curates. He seemed to have a sad capacity for turning even his greatest supporters against him, though it must be said, in fairness, that he was always as strict with himself as with anyone else.

As it happened, I only spent ten months in Rainham, before being moved again, this time to Sevenoaks, where once more I was junior curate. Ken Bell, from my own ordination year (but 12 years older than myself) was there, as well as Dominic O'Sullivan, with Phil Donnelly as parish priest (the year 2003 would have seen his 100th birthday). Father Donnelly was one of the kindest of men I have ever met, a lovely priest, in many ways just like a huge teddy bear. One year I managed to put two annual holidays together, to enable me to make an extended trip to Australia to visit my brother and his family. While I was away Phil Donnelly, realising my parents might be missing my regular

Tuesday visits home, rang them up to see that they were all right. He was that sort of caring man. Another example: he was taking Holy Communion to an elderly lady in a nursing home, out in the countryside part of Sevenoaks parish. 'It's springtime,' she said to him, 'but I don't suppose I'll ever get to see bluebells again.' That same afternoon he cancelled all his other appointments, got his car out and went back to the home, put the old lady in the car, and drove her around all the local country spots where there were bluebells! He really was a beautiful character. Although by nature conservative, he wouldn't stand in the way of my (or any parishioner) initiating some pastoral change providing I (or they) could make out a good case for it.

While at Sevenoaks I taught in St Thomas's School in Hildenborough. Back in the 1940s the only way Father Donnelly could get any kind of boys' Catholic school in the parish (the girls had a local convent school) was to start his own, and this he did. From early beginnings with one teacher and six boys in a hut behind the church, he purchased a redundant maternity hospital! It gave him great delight to go round the classes and ask, 'Hands up all those who were born at school!' Although fee-paying and lurching from one financial crisis to another, Father Donnelly would tell parents, 'If you can't afford the fees, pay what you can', and while this was the policy the school was always full – and with Catholics. Sadly, the then Archbishop decided this was not Catholic – but exclusively private – education and forbade any parish money to be put into the school, which meant that many parents had no option but to withdraw their sons and send them to local state schools. In order for Saint Thomas's to survive it had to take non-Catholics. But having a priest or two on the staff, and so saving salaries, helped the finances. So for eight years I took on the task of ramming Mathematics down young boys' throats.

I spent eleven years in Sevenoaks altogether, rising from junior to middle and eventually to senior curate again. But the Lord, it seems, was determined I should not become too proud, for, when I had been fifteen years ordained, Father Tom Quinn, a former missionary who had joined the diocese, was sent to the parish, and since he was once again my senior, for the third time I went to the bottom of the pile! Actually, Tom became a very good friend, and his time with Father Donnelly and me in Sevenoaks proved among the happiest of my years there. We used to laugh when he would come down coughing to breakfast and announce in his gentle Irish brogue, 'Ah sure, I don't think I'm long for this world!' Sadly, this proved prophetic, for Tom died in Sevenoaks at a comparatively young age a year or two after I left there – and still only a senior curate.

From Sevenoaks I went to West Croydon. Canon Alec North was parish priest there and his conservatism made Father Donnelly look like a rabid revolutionary in comparison! In Saint Mary's there were no lay readers, no special ministers at Mass, no ecumenical involvement. He too, in his own way, was a kind man. He was an excellent conversationalist and a practical man whom you'd love to have with you if wrecked on a desert island because he'd know how to provide food and shelter. He could also have had a shining career as a first-class cricketer had he not become a priest. However, it was impossible to speak to him about anything to do with the teaching of the Church; there was simply no common ground. He retired just a year after I went to West Croydon – I don't think I was the cause! – and Canon Garry Pierce, who was appointed to replace him, proved to be the first forward-looking parish priest I'd ever had. I learnt more from Garry in the following four years than I'd ever learnt during the previous seventeen put together, so I opted to stay on with him at St Mary's even though I could have received my own parish two or three years earlier than I finally did.

Altogether I'd been a curate for just under 22 years when, in 1985, I came full circle and was appointed parish priest here at St Margaret of Scotland, Carshalton Beeches, between Croydon and Sutton, just four miles from the very place where I had been born, and where I've been happily ministering for the last 18 years. The parish is small enough for me to know almost every-one – certainly all those who regularly come to Mass. It is friendly and family-like. Indeed we often refer to 'St Margaret's Parish Family' and, like any true family, the parishioners are supportive and helpful – to me, to be sure, but more importantly to one another as well. Indeed, I have now lived longer in St Margaret's Parish House than anywhere else in my life, and truly think of it as home.

Virtually all priests these days find themselves having to take on some kind of extra-parochial work or activity. 'Secretariat' appears to have been my destiny. I've already mentioned my having been (non-playing) cricket secretary, even when at school. As a curate I was conscripted to be secretary to various Boards of Managers and Governors of schools in different parishes where I served. And since coming to St Margaret's, I have been Secretary of the local Deanery for seventeen years; of my Diocesan Council of Priests for nearly fourteen and, since 2001, Executive Secretary of the National Conference of Priests; a job which I have not only found intensely interesting but which has also enabled me to forge friendships with clergy outside my own diocese, thus giving me an insight into ways of doing things which are different to my own, and into the varying cultures of the different regions, especially the so-called north/south divide within the two countries I'm involved with, England and Wales.

As a younger priest, I had been inclined to write off the NCP as a group of clerical left-wing trendies, unrepresentative of the English and Welsh priesthood as a whole. I still feel that may once have been true, but it is certainly not the case now. My visit to Glamorgan University as one of the Southwark representatives in the Millennium year was an eye-opener. All the participants were truly pastoral priests, priests who had the glory of God and the spiritual good of his people at the forefront of their discussions. There were no tearaways, no people with their own hidden agendas; just clergy working, for the most part, in ordinary parishes doing the ordinary work of the Lord. The atmosphere was prayerful. Naturally there were disagreements, but not in any uncharitable fashion. Everyone who had something to say, not only had the opportunity to say it but also received a ready hearing. And, lest there may still have been any doubt, the Standing Committee, one of whose members I became at the end of that same conference, declared, 'if there should still be any way in which the NCP is not fully representative of the clergy of England and Wales, then we are determined to fulfil whatever it may take in order to become fully representative in every sense of the word'. After thirty years, the National Conference of Priests has truly come of age.

However, the extra-parochial task that I have found the most fulfilling has been my monthly two-hour session of confessions at Westminster Cathedral. This began five years ago as a result of some correspondence in *The Tablet*. I volunteered, as I wrote in my letter to Bishop Stack (then administrator of the Cathedral), that: 'as a Southwark priest, who times without number have myself benefited from the Sacrament of Reconciliation in the Cathedral, yet whose own pastoral ministry for this sacrament, outside Holy Week and Christmas Eve, is called upon only in single figures per month, I wondered if in some small way I might help'. The offer was immediately accepted, but what I had then not anticipated – but am now so grateful for – was how much I myself would get out of this ministry. I had not realised before that the low number of confessions in my own parish (I'm sure many of my parishioners do go regularly to confession – it's just that, being a small parish, they like to go somewhere their voices are not so easily recognised!) meant there was a facet of priestly ministry that I had all but lost. My monthly stint of 40, sometimes nearly 50, confessions has enabled me to regain that ministry, for which I am profoundly thankful and, far from being a burden, I always look forward to the last Tuesday of the month, which is when I am usually on duty.

The changes that occurred as a result of the Second Vatican Council came quite naturally to me, although there were a few facets with which I was slower to come to terms than with others. For example, it took me a while to take collaborative ministry on board. That could have been because I am happy with my own company; I don't easily get lonely and, at that time, didn't feel I needed people round me. I certainly welcomed the liturgical changes and was very happy to implement them, though looking back to High Mass at Wonersh I had to admit there was something majestic about it. The greater understanding of the liturgy that Vatican II inspired has taught us much: for example, that all that incensing and bowing was a little pointless. But one can understand people's sense of loss at its removal, because it was so nobly performed! I wish I could say we have given up that form of the liturgy for the sake of something better, but all I can actually say is that what has replaced it is only *potentially* better, because – I have to admit – there are some parishes where their liturgy is absolutely dreadful, due almost entirely to lack of understanding on the part of the clerical leadership. There are innumerable strange ideas and foibles: an unwillingness to sing parts of the Mass itself, substituting this with a four-hymn 'sandwich' instead, often with totally inappropriate hymns and poorly worded intercessions – on one occasion I even heard one addressed: 'Dear Mary'!

However hard, or by turns however gently, I – and others who have a love of the reformed liturgy – try to point these things out, seemingly the message doesn't get through. Indeed the very word 'liturgist' seems to have become a term of abuse. No doubt you've heard the old joke 'What is the difference between a liturgist and a terrorist? You can negotiate with a terrorist.' This attitude is so sad, and, even sadder, it's the same in so many schools, surely the prime places for inculcating love of the Church's revised worship. For example, when I first came here to St Margaret's, the headteacher of the junior school in the next parish, which the majority of our own children attend, would ring me up at the beginning of each term, and book me for Class Masses, Year Masses, whole-school Masses and so forth, and throughout my first couple of years we had some very happy Classroom Masses. Then, for some reason, the Head had a change of heart and wanted instead only whole-year Masses in the big school hall. All the atmosphere and intimacy of the classroom was lost, Mass celebrated instead among a little 'island' of people gathered in this huge concourse. When I'd been at St Margaret's about seven years, I wrote a paper for the Head and the staff about what I felt ought to be done with the liturgy. I tried to make it positive and to offer helpful suggestions – I certainly didn't set out to upset anyone – but from then on, until the day he retired, that Head never again invited me to celebrate Mass in the school.

We don't have an obsessively modern parish here, but I do take a little pride in our liturgy, and I count it as a joyous achievement that I have got St Margaret's congregation to sing. When I first came, the main 9.30 Sunday Mass alternated between a folk group and a more traditional choir. When the leader of the folk group moved away, we were left with an 'empty slot' two (sometimes three) Sundays each month, but I refused to compromise on the full sung liturgy even if that meant, as it often did, unaccompanied singing. And for the first time the congregation realised that they could not simply sit and listen to other people sing – they had to do it for themselves. The glorious result was that they responded, and in so doing many of them discovered that they actually liked to sing. So too – little by little, though it took rather longer – the 11 o'clock congregation also began to sing. Three years later the folk-group leader returned from overseas to live in the parish once more and got a new group going, but by then, maybe not everyone, but a goodly core was singing at each of the Masses.

I've never had 'a low spot'; thank God. I don't think I've ever had a major crisis in the whole of my ministry. Of course I've experienced the death of both my parents, but I feel that I was prepared for that before it came. Even when I suffered a coronary ten years ago, I didn't rate it as a crisis. (Actually it was the most painless heart attack you could imagine; nothing like the melodramas one sees on television.) Yes, I regularly have 'mini-crises'; sometimes I wonder how on earth I'm going to get through the week ahead, but, sure enough, 168 hours later, I invariably find that I have.

While I wouldn't like to give the impression that celibacy has always been easy to cope with, as an *issue* it has never seriously bothered me. In the last few years, particularly, I've seen so many married people grappling with so many problems themselves – difficult children, school issues, financial worries, fear of redundancy, relationship problems – and, after listening to their *cris de coeur*, I always get a knowing look when I say to them, tongue-in-cheek of course, 'And still you think celibacy's the harder option!' The people for whom I really feel sorry, however, are those men who left the priesthood to get married, but then suffered the trauma of marital break-up. They have truly had the worst of whatever life can throw at them. Whenever anyone starts talking about celibacy, it's necessary to see where they are coming from. At Wonersh their concern was homophobia, in the literal sense of the word – 'fear' of homosexuality. The authorities were terrified of students forming relationships with other students, hence the draconian rules about not entering one another's rooms, only going out in groups of three or four, and the prohibition of what they euphemistically termed 'particular friendships'. After ordination the fear among diocesan authorities was of priests getting into relationships with women. Of course, over the years, many men had left the priesthood to marry, but it was only post-Vatican Two, and particularly after *Humanae Vitae*, that this became a sizeable leaching of priestly personnel. I don't think that we should put too much blame on Church authorities in those days for not foreseeing what problems were going to arise (any more than we should witch-hunt bishops nowadays for not having had hindsight twenty years ago over the child abuse problem). As with so many other facets of life, especially in the sixties and seventies, the problems, challenges and difficulties were completely new. Five of the thirteen who were ordained from Wonersh in 1963 have now left the priesthood, perhaps a fewer proportion than in many similar groups. Three I have not seen since. I have the feeling that they wanted to make a clean break from the past and all their former friends. Tony Castle and David Payne, on the other hand, I have seen a few times. I once made the suggestion to other members of my year that, for our annual reunion and get together, we should also invite those who had left the ministry. I was quite surprised that the idea wasn't endorsed. I was sad that anyone in our class had left the active ministry, but as old Corby (Monsignor Corbishley, Rector of Mark Cross) used to say, 'better a good layman than a bad priest'. I can't begin to imagine what advice I would give to any young man being ordained at present. Perhaps I am too old, perhaps my spirituality is insufficiently deep, perhaps the generation gap is just too big. Young men today are on a plane of studenthood beyond anything that we ever experienced in our day at Wonersh.

My final thoughts are that we are not allowing lay people their rightful role in decision-making levels within the Church. Way back in 1957 Pius XII addressed the Second Congress of the Lay Apostolate in Rome; the Second Vatican Council issued a document *Apostolicam Actuositatem* on the laity; the 1987 Synod was on the Laity and, in its wake, Pope John Paul II issued the encyclical letter *Christifideles Laici*. The theology of the Catholic lay person is all there; it has all been worked out, but, to the shame of the Church, it is not being put into practice. Two obstacles, seemingly insurmountable, are being put in its way. First, the vast majority of the laity simply do not know what is available to them – and many are quite happy not to know, only too happy to have everything done for them. The second obstacle – and I have to confess that I'm not entirely blameless here myself – is that too many clergy equate their position with authority, and authority with petty power. Sometimes I ask myself just how much of what I do can only be done by a priest. Absolutely strictly: celebrating Mass, hearing confessions, anointing the sick and, if duly delegated by a bishop, administering confirmation. Actually it is wider than that. Yes, there are counsellors and they do a wonderful job; there are eucharistic ministers and they too are invaluable in visiting the sick. But sometimes, there are people in need of counselling who are ready to talk only to a priest; there are sick people who long for a priestly visit. Nevertheless, there are any number of administrative jobs that I like doing, but which – if I am ruthlessly honest – could, and perhaps should, be done by someone other than myself.

I can foresee one model of a future Church in which a priest is no longer the leader *of* a parish but the chaplain *to* that parish (and maybe to another parish as well). Are there not others who could just as well take on the role of leader: a deacon, perhaps, or religious sister, or a well-known and respected lay person of long standing? People talk about a vocations crisis, but I often wonder whether the Holy Spirit is saying to us, 'You've got all that teaching about the laity and you're not putting it into practice. I'm going to *make* you put it into practice. I'm going to take your priests away until you do!' For many years now, I have been taking my annual holiday in The Gambia in West Africa and I cannot help contrasting our situation with theirs. The Gambia is the smallest country in Africa, only seven-tenths the size of Yorkshire (although being irregularly long and narrow one still has to travel immense distances over abominable roads)! The entire country is one diocese with about 34 priests, of whom I know every one. But the Church there really use their laity – 'use' them, that is, in positions of responsibility – and, as a result, the vocations are pouring back. When I first went out there fifteen years ago, the clergy were roughly half and half: half local vocations, half Irish Holy Ghost Missionaries. Now, there are only about six white priests left, all but two of whom are soldiering on, way past retiring age. Yet despite the smallness of the diocese, there are ordinations every year. Just a short time ago, four African priests were ordained in a single ceremony, all of them from that tiny country.

The vocations, I am sure, could come flooding back here too, but not without pain. It might mean the complete restructuring of the parish as we know it; it might mean us priests taking on a different role and a different kind of pastoral ministry; it might mean our shuffling off our (relatively) comfortable lifestyle. But if, at the beginning of this twenty-first century, we have the openness to accept all the implications of late-twentieth-century theology concerning the laity, I have no doubt that the priests too will return.

Séamus Hester

Canon Séamus Hester is parish priest of Our Lady of Ransom, and St Gregory's with St Agnes, Eastbourne, East Sussex, in the Diocese of Arundel and Brighton

My formal education began when I was five years old. In 1943 I went to St Paul's Primary School, Kilmurray, Co. Roscommon, which had recently been opened, accompanied by great celebrations to mark the occasion. Our teachers were excellent and really challenged us at all times. However, it was difficult for a country boy to study at home, especially during the long spring and summer evenings. All sons of farmers were expected to give a helping hand, cutting and stacking turf, weeding in the fields, saving hay, wheat, barley and oats, and making everything secure for the long winter months.

At 13 years of age I left national school and began attending a secondary school at Castlerea, a 5-mile cycle-ride each way from my home. At that time in Ireland, plenty of farmers were land-rich but had only a small cash flow. Generally, children stayed at their primary schools until the age of 14 and then left to go to work. The only pupils who went on for higher education were either the offspring of parents who had surplus money, or those on their way to the priesthood or a professional career. There were very few secondary schools for ordinary students, and I was fortunate to go to one of them, a school set up by Mary O'Flanagan. She had been left some money by an uncle of hers and was determined to use it to provide a general education for older children. She also caused a stir because she made it coeducational, which was considered a very advanced concept. She started the school in two rooms that she had acquired over a bicycle shop. Fifteen years later, when I joined it, the school was well established. Most students left at 16, but a friend called John Flynn and I stayed on to do the equivalent of A-Levels. It was a good education, which included Latin and French, so when I went on to seminary, I knew Latin.

John would quite often say to me, 'Let's go and join the Oblates.' 'Get lost!' I used to reply. Every month we had a priest come to our school looking for candidates – that, of course, was encouraged in those days. About the time of the examinations John's father died and, as he was the eldest of ten children, he had to go out to work to help support the family. That put paid to any idea of joining the Oblates.

I had no idea what I wanted to do. Everything I thought of I rejected: 'No, I couldn't do that.' Then one day I said to my parents, 'I'm thinking of the priesthood.' Their answer was, 'Sorry we can't help you. You'd better go and see the priest.' I was blessed with super parents, three brothers and one sister. My parents had a deep, strong, unquestionable faith. We were very good friends with many of the local priests and I've numerous happy memories of them. We lived in the curate's end of the parish; the parish priest had his own house and area.

So I went to visit our local priest for advice and help. Before I'd even sat down, he said to me, 'What seminary do you want to go to?' I eventually applied for a seminary place in the middle of August 1957, only to be told I would have to wait for a cancellation. However, I was given a place in St Kieran's, Kilkenny (where Joe Gill, from my home parish, was studying) and volunteered for Southwark Diocese. Many priests from my diocese in Ireland had applied to Southwark because there were no vacancies at home, and a number served there for ten years or more (others were being trained to work in Australia, New Zealand, England, Scotland, Wales and North and South America). A neighbour of ours, Sean Kelly, served very happily in Camberwell, southeast London for nine years. He told me that they were the happiest years of his life. When he was home on holiday he'd be around at our house as we were at his.

I found seminary life very difficult; it was so restrictive after the freedom of secondary school education. It started, for example, with a four-day retreat. By the third day, three students had left! In my innocence I asked the guy next to me whether we should leave as well. However, I knew that it was all part of the preparation required for the priestly life.

The summer before my ordination was remarkable. Nine of us students – seven deacons and two other seminarians – went on a tour of Europe. It cost us £36 each! It was my first time out of Ireland. We went over to Liverpool, travelled down to Dover and then across to France, Belgium, Holland, Germany and down the Rhine Valley. Then we went on to Rome. When we got there we couldn't, as planned, stay at the Irish College, because the rooms were being decorated for the Irish bishops coming to the Vatican Council. It was the summer of 1962! There was a great buzz in Rome at that time. Very few of us knew the meaning of an Ecumenical Council or Vatican Council, although we did have some lectures that tried to explain their significance. The talk was all about change. Pope John XXIII had opened the windows and the spring-cleaning was beginning. Changes in the liturgies, Mass in the vernacular, and numerous other ideas, were being floated by both seminary students and professors. In addition, each of our group had been allotted a country to study. I was given Monaco and was actually fortunate enough to arrange a meeting with Princess Grace – a stunning experience. We were also arrested by the police in Monaco for wearing shorts!

Back in the seminary during my last year, more and more questions were being asked. Would there be an end to lectures in Latin? What about the movements of the Master of Ceremonies during a Pontifical High Mass? Would celibacy become optional? There were so many questions.

After six years at St Kieran's I was ordained in St Mary's Cathedral, Kilkenny on 2 June 1963. My class had started with 36 students and finished with just 13 actually ordained as priests. There was the rather crazy idea at the time of having one's first Mass in the city where one was trained – not in your own parish, which was the local practice. I had 40 or more relatives coming to my ordination and first Mass, and they had to be put up for two nights in a hotel in Kilkenny. I will always remember the evening of my first Mass because that was when Pope John XXIII died. However, there were celebrations in my home parish to mark my ordination and the marriages of my brothers – Frank to Marie

Cunnane and Michael to Maureen O'Grady. Special permission was given by the local bishop to celebrate three Masses in the family home.

Sooner than expected I received a letter instructing me to be at Archbishop's House, Southwark on 16 August to receive my appointment. I met up with four other priests; Jack Madden arrived later. There was no special meal or any formal welcome; we were just told to report to the parish priest of the place where we were going, given the train times, and then it was goodbye.

My first appointment was to St John the Baptist, Brighton. The parish priest was Father Michael Costello, with Brendan Feeney and Victor Cook as assistant priests.

When visiting a family soon after I arrived in Brighton, a woman at the door asked 'Who are you?' I replied that I was the Catholic priest replacing Father Grogan. 'Get away,' she said, 'no one could replace Father Grogan!'

I had four reasonably happy years there in Brighton, although it was very much the old style of life. Apart from celebrating Mass, going to the Legion of Mary and visiting, my big job was to visit the Bingo Hall. I was the chaplain to the Sunday-night Bingo! Actually I didn't find it too bad, because they were lovely people and it gave me an opportunity to chat with them.

One of the difficulties at Brighton was that the housekeeper was the parish priest's sister, and she was a bit of a tartar. She would even occasionally refuse to let in someone you had an appointment with, deciding that they should see the parish priest instead, as I was not deemed mature enough to interview or instruct that particular person. After two years of this I'd had enough and went to the parish priest, exclaiming, 'Either she goes or I go!' 'Oh, I'll talk to her,' he said. I replied, 'You tell the people from the pulpit that they are very welcome to come to me or any of the priests.' Gradually she did improve.

I settled in quite well and quickly, but in the first week I had a rather sad experience. I went down the town and met a local Church of England vicar, so I stopped to talk to him, just as I would have talked to a Church of Ireland vicar in Ireland. As I was talking to him, he seemed very uncomfortable and ill at ease. A Catholic parishioner passed by and said, 'Sad to see our new curate talking to a heretic!' So we took the hint and arranged to meet for a cup of tea once a week in the Mercy Convent. I just couldn't understand it. He was invited as a special guest at my farewell party in 1967.

A few years later ecumenism was being openly mentioned and church leaders of all denominations were encouraged to meet and pray together. Bishop Butler was specially invited to come down from Westminster to speak to us on this topic. All the clergy of Brighton were invited but not all attended. However, there was a reasonable turn out.

While I was at St John the Baptist, John Metcalf was an assistant priest at St Joseph's, Brighton. We worked together on a project we considered important for the community, forming a branch of the Catholic Housing Association, which helped many young couples to buy their own homes.

Brighton was quite an exciting place to be in the sixties; every weekend there would be a conference or something interesting going on. Coming from a country place in Ireland to a major town was stimulating and I thoroughly enjoyed my time there.

On 28 May 1965 came very interesting news. The Diocese of Southwark was split into two, and the new Diocese of Arundel and Brighton was formed, with Bishop Cashman as its shepherd. I was suddenly, therefore, in a different diocese. In 1971 Michael Bowen became the new bishop of this young diocese after Bishop Cashman's death. On 21 December 1977 Cormac Murphy O'Connor succeeded Bishop Bowen, who went to Southwark as Archbishop.

From 1963 onwards, documents emanating from the Second Vatican Council began to be promulgated. In that year we had the Constitution on the Sacred Liturgy, and the Social Communication document. In 1964 *Lumen Gentium* was published. I have to say these documents meant nothing to me at the time. No clear guidelines were given to priests about what they should do, and there were no compulsory study days, which would have given us an opportunity to come to grips with such documents.

The priesthood that I trained for has changed dramatically. When I think of the philosophy behind my first years in the seminary and the changes that came about through Vatican II, I realise what a dramatic time it was to be ordained in 1963 as the whole emphasis shifted as regards liturgy, laity, priesthood and so forth.

There were gradual changes as well – for example the Mass in the vernacular; dialogue Masses; the reduction in fasting time before receiving Communion to one hour; ecumenical services; dialogues with local Christian leaders and their communities; the involvement of lay people and the introduction of parish councils. I well remember the first parish council meetings I attended. The agendas were always the same and the curates were told beforehand that they had to be silent – it was time to let the laity talk.

Of course, the big change was in the liturgy. I was enthusiastic about the innovations and longed for the time when we could celebrate the Eucharist facing the people. Those were very exciting years. Some parish priests were prepared to change; some reacted rather slowly.

What I particularly liked about the thinking coming through at that time was the ecumenical aspect. It was very special for me. I remember when my mother was ill how the local Anglican rector's wife had Masses said for my mother's recovery. In the old days our non-Catholic friends would tease us, saying, 'If you swear, you'll have to tell the priest on Saturday night.' We'd say in reply, 'And you have to go and spend long hours listening to a boring sermon on Sunday.'

In 1967 I moved to St Dunstan's, Woking, a very challenging parish. It was a difficult move, as my father had died in the May. He had only been ill for a short time, so his death was a great shock to me. I went as an additional curate. The parish priest was Jack O'Connor, who had lectured in Canon Law at the Seminary. We moved into a new presbytery and there were many exciting projects going on. I was there for seven years.

I was in Woking when *Humanae Vitae* came out in 1968. One Sunday morning the BBC wanted to interview parishioners on their views on this encyclical. The parish priest was on holiday and there was a crisis brewing about securing permission for this. We rang Bishop Cashman, who insisted that he was in charge, and no permission for interviews was forthcoming. It was a difficult time for parishioners, and for priests, because we were all hoping for change. There were a lot of young couples and young families in Woking, with a very active PTA and an 18-plus club, so a good many people were acutely interested in the outcome of it all.

St Dunstan's Parish was enriched by having three very good schools. Four Sisters of the Holy Infant Jesus order used to travel daily from Weybridge to teach in St Dunstan's Middle School. In 1965 they moved into the parish and then about 12 young sisters came who were in formation in spirituality and were attending colleges of education in London. They had a wonderful influence on the parish. There was also a large Italian community and each Sunday a Scalabrini priest celebrated Mass in Italian.

From Woking I went to Lewes, as a curate, where Father Denis Hayes was the parish priest. He was very good to work with, because he treated you as a human being as well as a priest, and he was genuinely interested in anything you did in the parish. He was happy to let me do the visiting. I'd go out early in the afternoon and be gone for hours until late in the evening because there were all these country villages to visit; lovely places like Ripe, Glyndebourne, Glynde, Barcombe, Firle, Selmeston and East Chiltington. Most of the parishioners were farmers and, having come from a farming background, I was well away. I loved it, absolutely loved it. There were a lot of Catholics working at Glyndebourne and I'd get invitations to some of the performances.

After I'd been in Lewes for about a year I was asked to be chaplain at the prison, an important chapter in my life. I found it very interesting; it was where I felt the Church should be. I would go in to visit most days for half an hour or so, just to be there for those in need. It was very easy to do that because the prison was near to the presbytery and I had the invaluable assistance of Sr John.

At that time a lot of prisoners who had served long sentences and were coming to the end of their term were sent to Lewes to do rehabilitation courses, prior to their release. I used to sit on the Lifer's Committee, and found this a rewarding experience for three and a half years. I worked closely with the C of E chaplain. Prisoners were referred to by their surnames, or really rude nicknames, but the chaplain and I preferred to use Mr . . . and then started to use Christian names. I also began the system of using the term 'chaplain's assistants' rather than 'prison visitors' for our helpers. I would give them a certain number of prisoners to visit in their cells.

A Catholic priest can do very little wrong in prison, because he is seen as coming in from the outside, bringing cigarettes and so forth. He is in a better situation than the Anglican chaplain who is regarded as being part of the establishment, holding a key position on the Management Board. Prisoners were careful what they said in his presence.

I had a very easy time, by comparison. I tried never to take the side of a prisoner or the authorities; I just listened to both. The prisoners needed respect as human beings. I met some very interesting people in prison; most were there because of money, drink or drug problems. There were also many on remand; most of them would get bail and we would never see them again.

Having completed five happy years in Lewes I was appointed in 1979 as parish priest in Thames Ditton, which is near Hampton Court and the Thames. It was a traumatic time for me because, while I was in the middle of this move, I learned that my mother back home in Ireland was dying. On my first weekend as parish priest, I was standing outside the Thames Dittton church when I was called to the phone, to be informed by the Matron of the Nursing Home in Ireland that I ought to come immediately. I got home just in time to be with my mother when she died.

My stay in Thames Ditton was a short one but I was very happy and enjoyed the pastoral work. I was only there nine months when Bishop Cormac asked to see me. I thought he was going to enquire about how things were going in my new parish, but to my surprise he said that he wanted me to go to Crawley, which had just been vacated by the Capuchin Friars. The Franciscan Capuchins had been in the Friary at Crawley for many years and had done great work, but age had caught up with them, and the area was ripe for pastoral and spiritual involvement. I was the first secular priest to be appointed to the parish of St Francis and St Anthony, known as the Friary, Crawley. My assistant was Robert Davies, and he and I lived in the 40-roomed monastery for three months. Then we acquired a mobile home.

The first big project was to build a presbytery. As a priest, I found it very hard. I was inexperienced and at that time there was still very little lay involvement in plans of this magnitude. To finance the project the parish sold land from the old Friary site. From the proceeds a new presbytery was built and we were able to build in addition three flats for retired priests and a house-keeper's flat. By the following year, times had changed, and five parishioners were closely involved in the building of the Friary Centre.

During this time Bishop Cormac then decided to amalgamate parishes and bring St Bernadette's in Tilgate under the Friary Parish. He was keen that all the Crawley parishes worked closely together in some form of team ministry, but as we had no clear guidance or experience of team ministry, we remained independent parishes, though we cooperated and worked closely together as best we could. We became a team of four priests, two Sisters and several lay parishioners, who were active in leadership roles. It was a new experience working with two highly qualified sisters – Mairead and Melissa. Another Holy Infant Jesus Sister, Catherine, invited us to attend a seminar on RICA (Rite of Christian Initiation of Adults) in London. As a result, we decided to go ahead with RICA in the parish of Sts Francis, Anthony and Bernadette, known as FAB! We worked as a team; we would meet every Monday and plan ahead, rotating the chairperson each week. Parish, hospital and school visits – both primary and secondary – were planned.

I was privileged to be in Crawley during the early preparations for the building of St Catherine's Hospice. The parishioners were very generous; I recall that one year, £7000 was raised at a parish function and that Daniel O'Donnell, the Irish pop idol, helped the parish to make another large donation to the hospice of £6000.

It was uplifting to be involved in a parish where so many became involved in pastoral and spiritual formation.

There are two very special religious communities close to Crawley. One is Worth Abbey, and over the years the abbots and community there have played a vital part in the Crawley deanery. Many deanery celebrations have been held in the new Abbey, as well as many ecumenical services. The monks give valuable guidelines on good liturgy and have often arranged lectures and invited excellent speakers. They have always extended a warm welcome to priests and religious, and to people from the Crawley deanery and beyond; and are hugely supportive, welcoming and helpful with supply when priests become ill or are away on holiday. The second community is the Carthusians, St Hugh's Charterhouse. The Carthusians are the strictest male religious order in the Christian world. They keep the vow of silence six days a week and rise every midnight to pray for two hours. The brothers use bicycles to move from one cloister to another because of the length and size of the monastery.

After seven years at Crawley, Bishop Cormac appointed me to St Joseph's, Brighton, where I was warmly welcomed by parishioners and Our Lady of the Mission Sisters. It is a lovely parish with lovely people, many of whom are young, due to the presence of two universities; that is where my pastoral involvement with students began.

Shortly after going to St Joseph's, Bishop Cormac launched the Renew process by celebrating Mass at the Goldstone football ground in Hove. Thousands of people came from all over the diocese, and the Renew process led to the formation of small groups, prayer groups, liturgy groups, and parish teams with individual members taking responsibility for various growth areas such as youth, ecumenism, liturgy, marriage and family life, social concerns and maintenance. The priests were free to give more time to spiritual matters and sacramental preparation, and at the same time to encourage parishioners to collaborate in building up the whole parish. The response to Renew in St Joseph's was great.

During those years of growth there were other important events. Ivor Pelling was ordained to the permanent diaconate and the RCIA process was developed. Many students were moving into the area with the expansion of the universities and there were great efforts made by parishioners to minister to them and keep in close contact with the university chaplains.

As a listed building, St Joseph's needed considerable maintenance, and a lot of time was spent raising money for the restoration work. The generosity of the people was remarkable.

In 1987, shortly after going to St Joseph's, the opportunity arose to go to Peru. I went for six weeks to visit the three priests from our diocese – Benny O'Shea, Ian Byrns and Hugh Dutton – who were working out there. David Rea and I first did the tourist bit – Cuzco and Machupicchu – then we flew to Piura and went on by jeep up the mountains to Frias. That visit to Latin America was the most interesting six weeks of my life.

I was very lucky on the flight out. We were flying via Paris and I moved from a non-smoking to a smoking compartment, exchanging with an asthmatic passenger. By great good fortune I found myself sitting next to a French passenger who spoke good English and knew Spanish; like me he couldn't settle or sleep during the 13-hour flight, so we spent the whole time in conversation, during which he tutored me so that by the time we touched down I could read the prayers of the Mass in Spanish. It was not unlike Latin, so it wasn't that difficult, once I had the pronunciation. It meant that I could concelebrate Mass, though I couldn't really speak the language.

We went out on mules and horses to meet the people in the campesinos, and slept – or tried to sleep – in barns. I remember one night when I was lying on some bales of corn I could hear the rats in the corner chewing on the corn! That was probably the worst experience of my life!

Each community living in the mountains hears Mass only

once a year, so our visit was very important to them. Everyone, just everyone, came out to meet Fr Benny and his two guests. There were many baptisms and marriages, and one Mass was said for all those who had died during the year. We baptised 99 babies one morning, and I remember in another place witnessing 14 couples being married. Catechising the huge numbers was the biggest issue. Willing volunteers were brought down from the mountains to be trained at a catechetical centre at Piura to become parish catechists. They then went back and prepared people for the sacraments and the annual visit of the priest; they held Sunday liturgies and the bishop or the parish priest would prepare a written sermon for every Sunday.

When after five weeks we returned from the mountains and came back down from Frias to Piura, we were so grateful to get back without accident. If you fell and broke your ankle you wouldn't get to a hospital for about a week. Earlier visitors had had to walk and climb; by the time we visited a road had been constructed and we travelled in a jeep that had been provided by the people of St Joseph's Brighton, so that was very special for me.

Meeting the people, with their simple faith, was hugely moving. One particular family sticks in my mind. I saw this couple sitting resting against a tree with their baby, outside the priests' house. One of the nuns was around who spoke Spanish so I asked her to interpret for me. Where had they come from, I asked? It turned out they had walked for two days through the mountains, and were wet through, having bathed in a local river after their long journey. Later that night I saw them still waiting outside, sitting with their backs to the tree, where they spent the night just waiting for Baptism, and I can tell you it was chilly at night-time. That was the sort of faith I witnessed. A typical conversation with a couple in Latin America, about their family was, 'four with God; four alive'. We saw a child's funeral, on one occasion, with only children in attendance. Children were carrying the coffin. The mourners were children. There were no adults.

When we came down to Lima, after the five weeks up in the mountains, I saw the newspaper headlines 'Storms sweep South

Coast of England'. It was in October 1987, the time of the great storms in England. When I got back I discovered severe damage to the roof of St Joseph's Church!

My happy years at St Joseph's came to an end in September 1999 when Bishop Cormac invited me to take a sabbatical. I decided to spend the first six months of my sabbatical at All Hallows College, Dublin. The lectures were mainly pastoral, but with some Theology and Scripture. I found myself with a group of nuns, some of whom had had bad pastoral experiences with parish priests. It was sad listening to their stories. They were headteachers, provincial superiors and others, who had not been permitted to organise even the simplest liturgical event. It was very much an experience of the Church of the past. Those who had been in missionary countries had experienced pre-Vatican II conditions and many sisters were ready for a sabbatical.

After six months on sabbatical in Dublin I contacted Archbishop O'Brien of Edinburgh, and went there. Actually, before I went I had a week at Knock, the shrine in the West of Ireland. It was Holy Week and very busy with confessions; people coming from all over, it being nothing to have 20 or more priests hearing confessions. That time was like a retreat for me.

Then I went to Edinburgh. The priest that I was to stand in for had undergone an operation and the archbishop wanted to get him into a nursing home, so I had care of two parishes: Duns which was inland and Eyemouth, a fishing port. I was able to see wonderful parts of Scotland; beautiful places like Loch Lomond. I loved it so much that I returned for my summer holiday.

During my time in Crawley Bishop Cormac appointed me to be the Director of the Diocesan Pilgrimage to Lourdes. It was a very challenging task but one I enjoyed for 23 years. It was a privilege to be so closely associated with the sick and disabled, their helpers, and able pilgrims from all over the diocese. After Edinburgh, then, I went to Lourdes, and spent five weeks there. I found it very different being based there rather than visiting for a week. I went to celebrate morning Mass at 9am for the day-pilgrims; people who travelled by coach, tour groups and the like. Then from ten o'clock until half-twelve there was the sacrament of reconciliation. After that, there was more time in the confessional from 2.30 to 6.00 – which is quite a long time to be hearing confessions – but we did have a break. I found it one of the most enriching experiences of my life being involved in helping to reconcile so many people to God. Young and not-so-young would come to make their peace with God and then go to the Grotto. There are so many people carrying unnecessary baggage and problems in their lives.

I was busy, but I loved the work. Friends in Lourdes gave me the use of a three-bedroomed flat, but I never once went into the sitting room! I was so tired at night that I went straight to bed. I was meeting people in a different capacity and was able to spend time with them, to stand and talk. So I saw Lourdes from a completely different viewpoint.

Then there were two family weddings, so I returned to Ireland. While I was away from the diocese, Bishop Cormac was transferred to Westminster as Archbishop and a year later Bishop Kieran was appointed as our new bishop in Arundel and Brighton.

Returning to the diocese I was asked to supply in Bognor Regis as Benny O'Shea, who was then parish priest there, had to have a hip operation. I was there during the time of the severe flooding and sometimes found it difficult to get to the outlying churches to say Mass. The diocesan authorities asked me to visit the retired and sick priests of the diocese, which was rewarding work. All of the retired were at different stages; some were very advanced in years, some quite recently retired. Some were ill, but none complaining about anything. They all had what they wanted in terms of accommodation and that included one priest who wanted nothing more than a comfortable chair, an ordinary bed and a kitchen table chair for a guest. That's all he required. 'I don't want any more furniture,' he said, 'I won't use it.' Some of the retired were living on their own, some in convents. Most of them, except the very sick, were still helping out in their local parishes by saying a Mass and helping with penitential services, being invited by fellow priests to lunch and still feeling needed and wanted. It did my priesthood enormous good to witness all that.

It was a great delight when Bishop Kieran appointed me to Our Lady of Ransom and St Gregory's with St Agnes in Eastbourne about a year after I had finished my sabbatical. A very warm welcome was given to me on my induction, which coincided with the centenary of Our Lady of Ransom. I've been very impressed by the daily spiritual life of so many of our parishioners, and the attendance at daily Mass. I am also impressed with the prayer groups, the rosary groups and the excellent attendance on Sundays. I have two parishes to look after and three churches. It's not that easy, but the people are very understanding about the fact that we are stretched for manpower. Lay involvement is very good, especially with sacramental preparation. I was blessed through having Fr Dominic to assist me when I arrived. Also in Eastbourne was Fr Joe Ware who was ordained in the same year as me. He had been involved in a serious car accident many years previously and was living with the Bergin family, cared for by Doreen, whose son Christopher is now a priest in the diocese. Joe has helped a lot, as does Geoff de Putron, who lives close to us at the presbytery and is always refreshing. Charles Howell came in September and is sharing the pastoral work with me. The presence of Our Lady of the Mission Sisters and the Dominican Sisters is a great blessing.

When I look back and reflect on my training for the priesthood all those years ago in Ireland, we had four months of freedom each year, out 'in the world' doing what we liked. A month at Christmas and three months in the summer; we had to be out of the seminary by the first week of June.

I think we could have been taught a lot of things that we weren't; for example about the spiritual life. We really weren't taught how to pray. We thought that the only prayers were the Our Father and the Hail Mary. Having said that, we had good discipline, but we were free. The Rector use to say, every Sunday, 'The gates are open, go any time you like.' It was perhaps more enlightened than the English system, but it could also be very strict. For example, after 10 at night you could not 'greet' anyone; if you were caught three times, you were out! We had a big turnover of students. Five went the first week I entered the seminary.

I know very little about seminary training today, and have very limited experience of it, but, from having had a deacon placed with me in my last year at St Joseph's Brighton, I would say that students must have as much contact as possible with the real life of parishes. Students should be living in presbyteries, seeing the day-to-day life of the priest, and just attending the seminary for their lectures. I'm not wholly for condemning the past; it was, on the whole, an enriching experience, but I do think we could do things better.

As for the present state of the Church, I would like to see more lay people involved in the ministries at every level. When Bishop Cormac was in the diocese he encouraged the creation of a team of lay people as an active pastoral team; people who would be the arms and legs of the priest, sharing responsibility for the parish. The diocesan feeling is that this is going to be done better in the future than in the past.

I really think that we have a far healthier Church today than we had 50 years ago. Then the parish priest, Reverend Mother and housekeeper controlled everything. A new parish hall, even a new church, would go ahead with no discussion. In parishes today there is more dialogue and collaborative ministry.

A gentleman recently asked me, 'When my grandchildren are grown up will there be a priest around? It's a great worry.' Someone else said to me, 'What kind of Church will it be?' I genuinely believe that the Holy Spirit is with the Church today and will be with us until the end of time. As there is much prayer for the future, whatever kind of Church we have, it will be the one God wants us to have. It may mean, for example, that the Church will decide to have married clergy, with the option, of course, of celibacy, for those who want it. Personally I don't sit back and think about the future, my concerns are for the present.

A highlight of my ministry, over the years, must be the prison work. I learnt so much about human beings; how so many good people can go down into the gutter through money, drink and drugs. The South American trip was another highlight. Working with the Sisters in Crawley, as a team where we were building on each other's talents, was a real growth experience. Being Director of the Diocesan Pilgrimage to Lourdes was an annual spiritual injection.

At the other end of the scale there were low points. Many a time I have asked myself at night, 'Why am I doing all this?' What I have found hard and unchristian is the way priests who have left the ministry to marry have been treated. I can't understand people's attitudes sometimes and have to walk away when they launch into tirades against them.

My sabbatical helped me to realise that I must be a priest of today. There is no point in brooding over mistakes I have made in my ministry. I've said things to people which have hurt them, when there was no intention of doing so; sometimes I've probably also been a little bit hard; but the sabbatical taught me to live in the present, to enjoy the present and not to go thinking too far ahead.

If I do think about the past, I must recall the deaths of Ken Snaith in 1991, Stephen Hinde who died in 1984 and the recent sudden death of John Medcalf in 2002.

A phrase used frequently during the lectures in my sabbatical year was 'you are watering the roots of your faith'. It was a reminder to go back to the very roots of my Christian faith, which came through the waters of Baptism. I hope and pray that as I give thanks to God for 40 years in my vocation as a priest, I may be granted some more years to continue to serve the Lord in his Church.

It is a well-known fact that parishioners in England have a great love for their priests. I pay tribute to the many families who have befriended me over the years. I firmly believe that it was the love and friendship of many parishioners, loyal and brotherly priests, the goodness and hospitality of sisters in various convents and, most of all, the guidance of the Holy Spirit that helped me to continue in the priesthood.

Finally, I thank my family – Frank, Marie, Maureen, Paudraig, Patricia, Anna, Willie and all my nieces and nephews – who welcome and support me in so many ways.

III
Retired members

Kenneth Bell

*At present Father Ken is cared for at the Wickham
Court Nursing Home, West Wickham, Kent*

It was for his love of music and the theatre, particularly the
opera, that Ken is best remembered by his confrères. His love of
music brought him alive, as those who benefited from the Music
Evenings that he put on will remember. Kevin Pelham recalls
that Ken took an active part in the annual Gilbert and Sullivan
operettas and plays, as the photo on page 140 bears witness. He
was also 'Charley's Aunt'. In the 1950s and early 1960s the Theatre
Law, forbidding clergy under pain of mortal sin and excommunication, was in force. It covered Shakespeare as well as West End
shows, opera and the ballet. For Ken, that meant making a very
big sacrifice to pursue his path to the priesthood (thankfully the
law was repealed in the late 1960s, in the light shed on legalism
by the Second Vatican Council).

Ken was a late vocation to the priesthood. He was born and
brought up in Clapham. On leaving school he went to work with
Cubitts in Westminster, where certain friendships fostered his
great interest in the classical music of particular eras. When he
made up his mind to enter the priesthood Ken spent a year
preparing in the presbytery at English Martyrs, Walworth, part of
which was devoted to this purpose. He then went on to St John's,
Wonersh. After his ordination Fr Ken was appointed to the St
Thomas of Canterbury parish, Sevenoaks, where, for a year or so,
he was a curate with Kevin Pelham. His next appointment was
back to English Martyrs, Walworth, where Fr Tom Power was his
parish priest. Towards the end of August 1977 Fr Ken was moved
to St John the Baptist parish, Purley, where Canon Denning was
his parish priest.

Fr Ken had only been in Purley for two weeks when he had a
near-fatal road accident in Islington. It was 8 September, and his
day off. He had, as far as can be ascertained, been visiting 'The

Screen on the Green' where his favourite old films were being shown. Crossing the road near Islington underground station he was knocked down by a car. At the time there was a great deal of speculation that it was a hit-and-run accident. This was evidently not true as the driver of the car stopped. The accident was dealt with officially. Ken was rushed to the intensive care unit at St Bartholomew's hospital, with a very bad head wound. It was generally believed that he would not recover.

Mass was celebrated for him, by Canon Denning, every evening at 8pm and the church was invariably full. It was at this time that Mrs Paulette Coldham began visiting Ken daily, although neither she nor her husband, Peter, knew him. 'It's a very long and complex story,' Paulette says of the following months and years. During the four months Ken remained at Bart's he was virtually unconscious. He was fed through a tube in his nose. There was little medical hope for his recovery. Paulette and Peter played Wagner and Mahler tapes, which the nurses left on; Paulette always spoke to him as if he could hear, introducing herself by name. Paulette adds that 'there is much to be told about this time'.

In January 1978 Fr Ken was moved to the Eastern Hospital at Homerton (which has since been rebuilt). The nose-tube was removed and a kind of forced feeding began, with great difficulties. Because of the very long journey across London from Purley to Homerton, Paulette and Peter were only able to visit once a week on a Saturday. On one of their visits, in February, when they arrived at the hospital another family, who had not seen Fr Ken since the accident, was visiting from Sevenoaks. Paulette and Peter decided to wait outside, but they were called in; Father Ken was uttering his first words, and asking for them by name. Even though he had apparently been unconscious he had been taking things in.

It was at this time that a Sacred Heart Sister, Patricia Collins, who was actually a teacher, found Ken on her regular visits to the ward. Seeing him in such a terrible state, almost unconscious and unable to move, speak or eat, she asked the nurse in charge of the ward who he was. When she discovered that he was a priest she obtained permission to take him Holy Communion and started caring for him. Paulette and Peter soon made friends with Sister Patricia and between them they were able to continue to help him.

During April of 1978, for several weekends, he was secretly moved to the Sisters of Mercy Nursing Home in Southwark, so that he would be nearer to his elderly mother, who found the journey to Homerton too difficult. Because of Peter's friendship, through the cathedral, with the Mercy Sisters, Paulette and Peter were able to visit Ken and take him to Mass at St George's cathedral. Although he was only just conscious, it was during this time that they realised he needed constant personal care, as he was very unhappy. In June, with Ken's agreement, Paulette and Peter started bringing him to their home every weekend. He was in a bad state and could not move or eat on his own. He weighed barely 6 stone, so lifting him was no problem. Ken was unable to stand, as many of his joints had become atrophied because of the lack of movement and the difficulty of physiotherapy.

It was decided in February 1979 to operate on his left leg, in order to straighten it. There was a fear of what the anaesthetic would do to his already damaged brain. Sister Patricia and Paulette visited the Royal London Hospital during a period of snow, ice and whiteout, with hot food, as the hospital kitchen staff were on strike. Fr Ken had plaster from his foot to his groin for seven weeks. When he had stabilised, Paulette and Peter were able to get him into their car by removing the front seat, in order to get him back to their home. Shortly after this, arrangements were made, both with the hospital and the archbishop, for them to look after Ken permanently in their home.

He was provided with a bed in the dining room, under the windows, and a chair in the corner by a radio and cassette player. Gradually, over the next few years, with a great deal of help, Ken relearned many things: how to put a cassette in the player; how to read, say his office and celebrate Mass and so forth. Father Martin Lee (now Canon Lee) had been appointed to the Purley parish to replace Fr Ken and he played an important part in helping Ken to recover his priestly life. He especially helped him with the Divine Office every evening and assisted Paulette and Peter to help Ken to say Mass again; first at home, then on Saturday afternoons in the church, with a dry Mass in the chapel.

After several weeks of therapy at Headley Court (a RAF rehabilitation centre) Ken was able to walk a little without his wheelchair. Then, much later, after another three weeks at The Garden Hospital, Hendon, he was able, with some difficulty to get upstairs, with someone helping him. Gradually he became able to move to his own room upstairs. He reached the stage of being able to celebrate Mass on his own, with a 'minder'. At first that was Peter, but gradually a rota of men was made up from the Purley parish. They came forward willingly to learn how to look after Ken, prepare the Mass for him and be there. During the 1990s and up until the time when he was tragically struck down by a stroke, in 1996, he was celebrating two parish Masses at the weekend (6.30pm on a Saturday and the midday Mass on a Sunday; also the 10am on a Thursday). Intellectually his brain was very bright, but physically and emotionally he had many problems.

Each year from 1979 up until the stroke, Paulette and Peter were able to take Father Ken, with his wheelchair, away on a holiday, usually abroad. In 1979 and 1980 they travelled with a group to Italy to stay at the summer school of the English College at Palazzola, situated on Lake Albano, opposite the Papal summer residence at Castel Gandolfo. They also visited Makarska in Croatia, Medjugorje, Crete, Switzerland, Austria, Israel and many places in Italy, including Lake Garda, Lake Vico and Venice.

Once he had sufficiently recovered from his accident, Ken was very faithful to his priestly duties and prayer and the Daily Office were important to him, taking up most of the day.

After the stroke in 1996, Ken was taken to Mayday Hospital, Croydon. Needing constant nursing care he was moved to Wickham Court Nursing Home, where daily Mass is available. Among others who visited Ken, Pat Moloney recalls how they used to give each other a blessing. Slowly and sadly, Ken's health deteriorated until he was unable to read and his memory became so very poor that he could not recognise most visitors. Today he needs total nursing care, even feeding. Fortunately he still recognises Paulette, who is able to visit three or four times a week. She is still known as 'Mummy' by all the staff, as living with the Coldham family, Ken became 'one of the children'. Sometimes, now, she is even introduced as 'my mother' by Ken, which causes some confusion to new staff.

Paulette very often reads evening or morning prayer with Ken and is able to pray with him. Sometimes she reads a little from John Henry Newman's biography or from Graham Greene, or they listen to music together. Chatting is not easy because Ken finds talking difficult, but with patience it is possible to understand him, although he is sometimes confused. Occasionally he asks how he came to be in the Nursing Home and listens intently to his life story. He sometimes does not recognise his own room, but always does so when he is shown the crucifix over his bed, which was given to him by the visiting chaplain (name unknown) at St Bartholomew's, when Ken was unconscious in the W. G. Grace ward. He has been promised that the crucifix will always hang over his bed. He knows clearly that he is a priest; and he is much loved.

Joseph Ware

Father Joe Ware is a retired priest of the Arundel and Brighton Diocese

Joe Ware, born 1932, was almost killed in a car accident in 1984, while parish priest of Heathfield, East Sussex. Since 1986 he has lived with the Bergin family, who still care for him. He has little memory of past events. The following comes from an interview conducted in August 2001.

My family originally came from Brockley, in South London, although I was living at St Mary Cray, Kent, when I went to the seminary. My mother's maiden name was Dodd, which I believe is an Irish name; certainly the whole family were Catholics. My mother's brother, Father Henry Dodd was a priest of the diocese, but he died some years ago. I am the eldest of four sons. I went to St Mary's College, Sidcup and from there I went into the Royal Navy, straight from school. I was a boy sailor on *HMS Cleopatra*, a light cruiser, at the time of the Suez crisis. I'd always wanted to be a priest so when, after six years, I left the Navy, I went to Wonersh. I was perfectly happy with life in the senior seminary. After the discipline of the Navy, I had no trouble in settling in. I can't remember now whether I was involved in any of the community activities or not.

My first appointment, after ordination, was to Blackheath, where Alan Clark was the parish priest; he was, later, the bishop of East Anglia. I got on well with him and the other priests. I'm not sure now what parish I was in when I had the accident.

I've been living with a family for some time. I celebrate Mass every day; sometimes on my own and sometimes I concelebrate in the local church. My priest friends see that I get to all the big 'dos' in the diocese.

I can't really remember now where I went after Blackheath. I do remember that the changes from the Second Vatican Council were coming through and I had no problem about them.

I was sad to hear that Dave Payne, Sean O'Callaghan and Tony Castle had left the ministry. If a man has to leave, then that is what he has to do, but it is sad. If I were giving advice to a student preparing for the priesthood now I would recommend more personal prayer; I would say, 'concentrate on building up your personal prayer'. If we want to get more young men into the priesthood we've got to encourage children and young people to pray more; prayer will lead them to a vocation. I was involved in Opus Dei as an associate member, which helped me a great deal with my prayer-life.

I think one of the reasons for the crisis in the Church is that priests are not encouraging the people to develop their personal prayer-life enough. For me personal prayer came first and public prayer developed and grew out of it. There's nothing more important to me than the daily Mass and personal prayer.

Talking of the present crisis in the Church, we could involve the laity much more, but I've got some hesitation about the idea of married men as priests. I was brought up to believe that priests had to be celibate and that's how I feel it should remain.

I've no memory at all of my accident. I only know about it because people have told me it happened. I'm quite content with my life as it is; I have no complaints at all. My only conscious difficulty is trying to adjust myself to all the modern electronic things that there are around these days. I'm constantly surprised by things like mobile phones and video recorders.

The following additional information was supplied by Mrs Doreen Bergin, who, with her family, has been caring for Father Joe since March 1986.

After his first parish of Blackheath, Fr Joe worked from 1965 to 1970 in the parish of Our Lady Immaculate at Uckfield. From there he moved to Haywards Heath where he served with Father Byrne; Timothy Rice was the other curate. Father Joe got his first appointment as parish priest in 1977; to St Theresa's parish at Southwick, West Sussex. After six years he transferred, in February 1983, to St Catherine's parish, Heathfield, East Sussex.

Driving back to Heathfield from the 9.30am Mass at Burwash on Friday 9 November, Fr Joe's car was in collision with a lorry that had jack-knifed in front of him. Very seriously injured, he was taken first to Eastbourne hospital, but transferred almost immediately to the neurological unit of Haywards Heath hospital. For two weeks he remained in intensive care and had to have an emergency tracheotomy because he contracted pneumonia. He was transferred back to Eastbourne hospital where he remained in intensive care for a further four weeks. Due to the attentions of Dr Maureen Tudor, Fr Joe was sent to the RHHP hospital at Putney in April 1985; prior to this he had spent three months at Mount Alvernia hospital – run by the Franciscan Missionaries of the Divine Motherhood – at Guildford.

Much improved, the hospital informed the bishop in January 1986 that Fr Joe would regress if he stayed any longer in hospital. Doreen Bergin and her family, who had known Fr Joe for many years, agreed to take him into their home for a trial period of three months; the move was made on 14 March 1986. When the family moved from Burgess Hill to Eastbourne Fr Joe went with them. His health continued to improve, until it hit a plateau where it has remained.

The young driver responsible for the accident was deeply distressed by the event. He went with Mrs Bergin to visit Father Joe in hospital in Putney. He was readily forgiven and there is a photo of Father Joe giving the driver a blessing.

Doreen says of Fr Joe, 'His Faith is everything to him. The Mass is the be-all and end-all of his life. And he is intensely loyal to his brother priests, whose company he always enjoys. We take him on regular pilgrimages to Lourdes and when we went to Rome Fr Joe met the Pope. He is so proud of the photo of him with the Pope taken in 1995.'

Doreen Bergin's son, Christopher, decided to apply for the priesthood while studying Law at university. His mother was unaware of this at the time. Asked by the bishop to write an essay on his reasons for applying, Christopher stated that one of the principal influences upon him was the fine example of Father Joe who had lived with his family for many years. He is now a priest of the Arundel and Brighton Diocese.

Patrick Moloney

Father Pat Moloney who has recently retired, was formerly parish priest of St Joseph's, St Mary Cray, Kent, in the Archdiocese of Southwark

I was born in a room over a public house in Limerick, Ireland! My father was the publican and we lived on the premises. Having no brothers and sisters, and losing my parents at an early age, I suppose I have been disposed to the single life. My father died when I was approaching nine. Sadly I have only scattered memories of him, although they are all very happy ones. I have sometimes quoted him, when speaking on marriage. I tell of the time when I was about seven, and I was going on holiday with my mother. My father couldn't come with us because he was working. He told me what a special person my mother was and how I was to take good care of her. I was to hold her hand when I took her across the street and stay close to her when in the sea. Years later I realised how that incident showed how much he loved her. He was quite a spiritual man; the three of us said the rosary together every evening and my parents went to daily Mass.

Life was simple in those days. We lacked many of the modern comforts of life, but we didn't notice it because everyone in our community was much the same. I grew up in the same place only a little later than Frank McCourt who wrote *Angela's Ashes*.

Most of my primary education was at a little private school, just down the street from where we lived. The last three years of primary school and my six years of secondary education were spent with the Jesuits in Limerick, and at the Crescent College (well-known contemporaries were Richard Harris and Terry Wogan).

One day I was very flattered when three of us were called out of class to meet the Jesuit Provincial. At first we were worried because normally you were only summoned from class if you were in trouble, but we were taken because staff thought we had potential as future Jesuits! I cowered away from that suggestion, the idea not in my mind at all. The Jesuits and school were closely linked in my mind, and I didn't like school. Eventually we all become priests, but only one a Jesuit.

I left school at the age of 18 having passed my A-Levels and Matriculation exam. Of course when the results came out the pressure was on: 'What are you going to do?' I was sure about only one thing; I didn't want to work in the pub. My mother had tried to keep the business going, after my father's death, and it was assumed that I would take over the business. But I'd had enough of washing glasses and serving behind the bar.

In those days, in Ireland, most boys at some point would say that they were thinking of the priesthood; this is what I now declared. So, in mid-August 1957, I applied to All Hallows Seminary, Dublin. Going on to a seminary was not unusual at that time. I had half a dozen cousins who were either priests or nuns. Everyone knew someone who had gone off to the seminary, but I was disappointed to get a letter back from All Hallows telling me that the seminary was full so my name had been put on a waiting list for the following year! The idea of going to Dublin, the big city, to study was very attractive for a lad from Limerick. As a schoolboy I had saved up to go there, to stay in hotels and go to the theatre by myself. We lived in a more innocent world in those days.

I confided in a cousin, who was a priest, and he suggested the seminary at Thurles, County Tipperary, only about 40 miles from Limerick. That was less attractive, but it was a seminary. Thankfully I just got in. The seminary was so full that one year my bed was virtually in a corridor! There were 24 of us in my class at the start. A few left, and one or two were advised to leave; a few more joined us as we progressed through the six years; so 24 were ordained together in 1963.

During our first two terms, English and American bishops, and in fact bishops from several countries came coaxing us to join their dioceses. The American bishops particularly were strong salesmen. 'Come to my diocese,' they would say, 'it's the best in the world because ...' Most of my classmates chose American dioceses; it was also my first choice. If you had been to the cinema as often as I had, everything about the States was attractive. It surprises me, now, that students would make a commitment to a diocese thousands of miles away, of which they had no experience. Most of the class had never been out of Ireland before, following their ordination, they went off to the USA, Australia and South Africa. One day the seminary president called me up to see him. 'I believe you are an only child,' he said, 'that it's just you and your mother. You may have second thoughts about being as far away as the States. If you were to work in England, you could get home easily to visit your mother. Maybe you'd like to reconsider your decision. Incidentally, I promised the Bishop of Southwark that I'd find a student for him this year!' It embarrasses me now, but when you are eighteen you don't think much about your mother's future. So, with a degree of reluctance, I agreed to go to Southwark. At least the diocese included part of London.

Two of my classmates came with me to Southwark. One was on loan from an Irish diocese. The other suffered from poor health and returned to the Limerick diocese after a year.

In my time at the seminary we were only allowed home at Christmas and for a summer holiday; mid-June to mid-September. Just before the June exams, at the end of my second year, my mother wrote to me saying that she was going into hospital for an operation and it would be necessary for me to give my written consent. I received permission to visit her and travelled by bus to Limerick. I saw my mother in the ward, as they prepared her for the operation, and then I went to see the doctor. Imagine my shock when he said, 'Your mother will be dead in September.' It took my breath away, but I had to return to my mother in the ward, afterwards, and pretend that I'd heard nothing!

September came and it was then that the cancer began to affect her lifestyle. So I didn't go back to the seminary. She died on the last day of that year, New Year's Eve. On the face of it those final few months might sound miserable and pathetic; an only child, leaving the seminary to nurse his dying mother, with the pub business going down the drain, but I can honestly say that it was about the happiest time of my life; a very special time. Although I ended up the one injecting morphine, every four hours, it was above all a very loving time. My mother hadn't been very demonstrative of her feelings, but things changed as the days, weeks and then months passed, and I came to deeply appreciate all I had received from her. A worry she had also brought home to me how much she had loved my father. My mother thought that I, as a seminarian, had the answers to all religious questions, so she confided her concern that she was looking forward more to being with my father than to being with God! I reassured her as best I could.

In Ireland funerals take place quickly. I contacted the seminary to let them know and was told to be back for the first day of term. I had ten days to sort out such things as the future of the pub, which as a business was already disintegrating. So I returned to the seminary and was informed that the Bishop of Southwark would allow me the year if I made up the work of the lost term and passed my exams by Easter. Having no time to grieve properly was to have repercussions later in my life. Many years later, during training for bereavement counselling, I recognised in myself the symptoms of unresolved grief. It became evident to me that when my father had died I had been whisked away to a neighbour's home, and not really been a part of what went on. Then, when my mother died, I had only ten days to look after the funeral, sort out the business and get myself back to the seminary, to catch up with an extra term's study. Over the years since then I had been to many funerals at which I was more upset than the deceased's family present.

I look back to my seminary days as a wonderful time; my friends became my family. Having a home in Limerick provided a very convenient location for classmates to come and stay at my place; an opportunity for them to come into the city from the country; and they would reciprocate, I going to them. It gave me a good social life, what with the countryside, hunting, swimming, and so on. I got to know their families and they got to know me. While others seemed to criticise the seminary and the staff, I actually liked it. I can look back now and recognise that, for me, it was a substitute family, a good circle of friends, who are very important to me.

The day of my Ordination was the most special day of my life. The ceremony was in the beautiful cathedral of the Archdiocese of Cashel in Thurles. The only sadness was trying to hide a few tears at the end of the ceremony when the 23 other new priests went forward to bless their parents and immediate family – and I had none! We were allowed to invite 16 guests and that meant a difficult choice, but places were limited because the small town of Thurles had to provide accommodation for 24 different receptions after the service.

The Bishop of Southwark visited Thurles (and the five other seminaries in Ireland) each year and told us we would have three months free before he would call us to the diocese – we used to call it 'the sacerdotal honeymoon'. I took him at his word and went off to the United States, for two glorious months. I had a month visiting various relatives whom I hadn't met before. The other month was spent at St Augustine's Parish in Florida on 'holiday duty'; the emphasis was very much on the holiday and I was away most of the time. I was taken to visit the Gulf coast; a parish car and driver were provided to take me to drive the Atlantic coast to Miami and Key West. It seemed to me that all the rectories had Irish priests, some of whom I knew. It gradually dawned on me that I was being wooed to stay. It was all very glamorous and attractive but I had made my commitment to Southwark.

I have always loved to travel and as a student had hitchhiked around Western Europe with a fellow seminarian. I can still remember how, on my arrival at Holyhead, I was surprised to see a large poster advertising Post Office Savings with a lovely girl, in a spangly costume, on a trapeze. The slogan was 'Keep a good balance'. The Post Office in Ireland didn't advertise like that! I had visited London before, but going to live in England was going to be different and my introduction to the diocese would be a challenge. One of my classmates was on loan to Southwark from an Irish diocese and we flew together from Shannon. Attired, of course, in our black gabardine coats and hats, we arrived at Heathrow, early September, on a very hot day. I had two large suitcases and a bundle of books, tied up with string. We were advised to get the bus to the West London Air Terminal, and find a hotel. We dragged our suitcases and bundles of books around the streets on what was to prove a very exhausting afternoon. It was the height of the holiday period and all the hotels were full. My friend had never been to England before and he was getting increasingly concerned. I'd been twice to London and was a little more confident. We'll have to sleep in a doorway, I thought, my main concern about that being turning up looking scruffy for the meeting the next day with the bishop! We did eventually, though, late at night, get into the Cromwell Hotel. My friend didn't want to stay there because he didn't like the name 'Cromwell' – not a welcome name to Irish ears!

The next day we arrived at Bishop's House, and met no bishop. There was someone waiting for my friend, and he was taken to his parish. I was informed that whoever made appointments was away and wouldn't be back for a month. I was asked if I had any friends or relatives in London, with whom I could stay, but I knew no one in England! I spent a very long day in a small waiting room, with a little food at lunchtime. At about 6pm I was told that a taxi would take me to a nearby parish.

I had no idea where I was going and the taxi driver couldn't easily understand me; neither could I understand his cockney accent! However it was only a short journey. The taxi dropped me off, together with my two suitcases and the bundle of books, outside a church, which had its windows broken and bushes growing out of the gutters. I asked the taxi driver if this was where he was told to take me. He appeared to take pity on me and we walked together up to the front of the church, where we found a big 'For Sale' sign. I was very surprised. The taxi driver said, 'I think there's another church at the other end of this street; let's try that one.' It proved to be the right address. A curate opened the door and invited me in. Years later, Archbishop Michael Bowen told me that he was that curate and hadn't had the heart to tell me that no one was expecting me!

I was a lodger in the house beside the presbytery for my first month and I remember sending to Ireland for money. The parish priest was welcoming and helpful and we remained friends until his death. I related well to one of the curates, who was Irish, but I felt daunted by all the things he did. He ran a football club, a youth club and such like, and kept numerous lists, and files that I had never associated with priesthood – I hoped I hadn't made a mistake! I did help a little in the parish. One thing I particularly remember is the first time I heard confessions and the first penitent confessed in Irish! In those days the clergy were not allowed to go to theatres but as I held no official appointment I availed myself of 'my last chance' and went to many plays. I saw the sights of London, but I was very conscious of my black suit and clerical collar. It was a pleasant month.

Eventually I received my appointment to an island parish. The parish priest met me at the station and took me directly to the pulpit in the church! There were no microphones then and he wanted to hear me speak. I didn't have much to say . . . He and his sister, who was the housekeeper, made the presbytery a very happy home and I'll always appreciate their kindness. The church was named St Henry and St Elizabeth; someone in Ireland advised me to check that I was in the right place, as it didn't sound very Catholic!

Everything about life was new, different and exciting. For the first time I was meeting people who were not Catholics; it was a novelty to me.

The parish had a prison. When I first met the governor he informed me of the rules: you didn't take anything in and you didn't take anything out; you kept your distance and didn't get too involved. So imagine my surprise, on my first Sunday morning, when a young inmate came up to me, with a very friendly attitude. 'Surprised to see you,' he says. 'Moloney isn't it?' I thought, how does he know my name. 'You're from Limerick, aren't you? Roches Street?' None of that information could have come from the governor; but the young man really did know me. As a young boy he had come regularly to our pub with his father – he having a bottle of lemonade while his dad had his pint – and he had seen me serving behind the counter. Sometime after he left prison I was flattered when he brought his girlfriend to meet me and asked my opinion of her! Years later I met him by accident in Piccadilly Circus and he was shopping for a gift for his daughter's First Holy Communion; so all was well.

After five happy years I moved from my first parish. I'd got to know very few other priests. The next parish was just along the north Kent coast. The afternoon I arrived I was subjected to what amounted to an interview in which I felt I didn't do very well; my answer was repeatedly 'no' to all the questions. 'Do you type?' 'Can you drive a mini-bus?' 'Do you have your own car?' 'Can you play the organ?' 'Have you scouting experience?' I was also given the rules of the house – for example, 'the kitchen is out of bounds; you will be expected to be out all day on a Wednesday'. I felt really sorry for myself, as it was October and I wouldn't be able to afford to go up to London every week. What would I do? Again the parish priest had his sister as housekeeper and his mother also lived there. I lived a very independent existence and had a separate entrance to the presbytery. After a few months and a lot of walking, especially taking Holy Communion to the housebound, I was given the use of a parish car. I was given a lot of freedom to do whatever I thought appropriate and, with the support of the Sisters of Mercy, it was another happy four years, thank God!

Changes in the Church were beginning to come through after the Second Vatican Council, but I'm glad to say that I don't remember any particular stress. Celebrating the Mass in English and facing the congregation for the first time was no real problem. Amusingly I remember someone apologising to me just before I left the parish – she said she had never liked me because she thought that having the Mass in English was my idea and had only just discovered it was happening everywhere! Our catechesis must have been very poor.

The next parish was away from the sea but close to London. It wasn't the happiest of presbyteries and again there was a lot of walking until I got money from Ireland to buy my first car. With no car allowance I soon discovered how expensive a car is to run! (There were many discrepancies in those days. For example, just as some assistant priests had to surrender funeral stipends to parish funds while others didn't, so some curates got a car provided, some were helped to buy their own, while the lucky ones got a car allowance.)

I remember an elderly lady telling me that I was the only person in her life who called her by her Christian name. That gave me a sensitivity to the fact that nobody in my life called me by my Christian name – I was always 'Father'. That's a great impoverishment.

Some priests, serving in Southwark, had returned to Limerick and I considered doing the same. I also thought of volunteering to join some cousins and friends working in South America; but I realised that I would not be doing so for the right reasons. I always liked visiting people in their homes and in my new parish was given freedom to do this. After four years I asked for a move, as my doctor had indicated that certain physical ailments I was suffering from were down to stress. It took another year before I was moved.

A whole new life and whole new world! I was appointed to Thamesmead, and my time there was to prove a blessing. I had the novel experience of being interviewed by six members of the team ministry, led by Jim Thompson (later bishop of Stepney and subsequently of Bath and Wells. He was truly gracious, inviting me to Christmas dinner with his family on my first Christmas there). It was exciting to belong to an ecumenical team. (In my early years in the priesthood I had started going to clergy fraternals – regular meetings of the local clergy – and was increasingly grieved by the lack of Christian Unity.) At its full complement, the team comprised eight ministers from four different denominations. I attended the team meetings, but must have been there six months before I opened my mouth. The meetings lasted three hours, from 8.30 to 11.30am every Friday morning. It was a high priority; no funerals were accepted at that time, nor school assemblies. Each member of the team had a personal assessor, and each of us was regularly assessed. That sounds a bit threatening but in fact it was very supportive. It was a huge change; going from five years in a place where I didn't even answer the telephone, to living on my own in a flat in a tower block. Perhaps I idealise the past somewhat, but I look back to my time in Thamesmead with great nostalgia. No church, no hall, no regular presbytery; just a one-bedroom flat in one of 18 identical tower blocks. I felt that I was a full-time priest; nothing to do but be with people. There was no property to maintain and the diocese paid the rent. This made me very attracted to the early history of the Church, when they had no property. Now we have the millstones of churches, houses, halls, schools, grounds and so on round our necks.

On Thamesmead I could say that I had a working relationship and a friendship relationship that were new to me. The team-work and the assessment process, both involving sharing with the others, were equally new. These offered a level of profession-alism and a certain accountability that proved very helpful, but most helpful of all was the support they brought.

There was a very high level of student placement in Thames-mead, from a wide range of backgrounds; social work students, medical students and so on. There were also Anglican Church students, but it wasn't until my last year that four Catholic students, from Wonersh, were placed there. It was viewed as a quite progressive place to be. As a Local Ecumenical Project we had permission to do 'new things', such as a simultaneous Eucharist on Sundays.

Sunday morning Mass was celebrated in the primary school, many other events also being held there. There was a Sainte Union sister as headteacher and we worked really well together.

All the parents were parishioners and almost all the parishioners were parents; it was a very young congregation. I used to delight in the liturgies such a flexible space made possible. You could plan a liturgy involving everyone in a way that simply wasn't possible in a traditional church setting. The school hall had coloured lights and dimmers, meaning that an atmosphere could be created very easily. Marriage Encounter was well established in the parish and this, also, was something new and enriching for me. All of the above – working with the Team, the vibrant liturgy and Marriage Encounter – significantly broadened my horizons. I had five very happy years in Thamesmead.

My next appointment was as parish priest. Looking back I made it heavy going for myself. I was 'too busy' to take a day off. There were building problems – dry rot, wet rot; you name it, we had it – in the presbytery and school, and I took these too much to heart. I'd felt a full-time priest in Thamesmead, but as parish priest it was more like being a property manager.

After seven years I was moved to a bigger parish; by that time I was more relaxed as a parish priest. It was a delight to have so many laity involved in the life of the parish – we had 32 different groups. There had been three priests in the parish, and the workload was heavy with two of us. Again there were property problems! A major project involved the demolition of two old schools and the building of a new one costing £3 million (at that time). We were blessed with very competent school governors and much hard work was done liasing with the government and local authorities; however there was still a great deal of worry over architects, builders, neighbours and so forth. Eventually all ended happily.

The 'Parish Project' was a huge exercise in discerning the needs of the parish, and training people in lay ministry and for the parish council. It was good to have an assistant priest and, yet again, the help of a Religious sister, this time of the Blessed Sacrament Congregation. She helped me to appreciate more a woman's ministry. We were flattered when *The Universe*, a Catholic newspaper, sent a reporter and photographer to present a feature on the parish as a model of 'collaborative ministry'. This produced a number of letters from around the country and we were pleased that what we had tried to do had been affirmed. I was increasingly spending my 'free day' in bed, attempting to catch up with lost sleep so, after seven years, I was pleased to have a sabbatical.

I am very happy where I am at present and with my present parishioners but again there are property problems! The Permanent Diaconate was discussed at our regular Deanery meeting of priests and I proposed the idea of an experiment whereby the younger deacons, with their families, move into some of our larger presbyteries to take on the full administration and responsibility for a parish. In the past month I've had two break-ins, another leak in the church roof, a leaking central-heating system in the hall, a broken fence and damaged grounds, and I'm in dispute with Thames Water. Priesthood can be flushed out by property problems!

Sometimes I fantasise about retiring – like normal people – when I am 65. A wilder fantasy is of ending my days in some religious community! I have never wanted to be anything other than a priest and would always want some priestly ministry – I couldn't be a shepherd without a flock.

Looking back over 40 years I'm very grateful for the parents I had and for the love of God and the Church which they gave me. My father once corrected me for putting six pennies on the collection plate in our Augustinian church and not the silver six-penny piece that he had given me. He told me that coppers were never good enough for God! I am very blessed with a wide circle of friends whom I contact regularly and with whom I spend my holidays – in different countries. (As I've said, travel and leading pilgrimages to various places always give me great pleasure.)

I am also very grateful for my six years in the seminary – where we were expected to pay for ourselves, if we could afford it. The training was probably deficient in various ways, for example, in the use of Latin textbooks by ancient authors. I visit my seminary in Thurles at every opportunity and defend it if I hear it criticised.

The training of priests has, of course, changed beyond all recognition. A few years ago there was a study day at Wonersh, the senior seminary, to help us to understand the more recently ordained priests. It helped me to appreciate that students today come from a very different world and are being trained for that world. Our training was for the world as it was nearly a century ago – the pre-Vatican II world. Hopefully we have adjusted.

The Church in our part of the world is certainly going through a rough time. Much needs to be done to learn from past mistakes, but I am confident that there will be a healing of hurts and a forgiveness of wrongs. I find it discouraging when good people put so much time and effort into various projects with little results. One wonders when the seed sown will bear fruit. I suppose every parish has wonderful lay people who do more than their fair share, and we can all be challenged and encouraged by them and their goodness.

Parish visiting doesn't happen much these days, because there are fewer priests and most houses are empty during the day. If there is an opportunity to visit in the evening many people are reluctant to open their door after dark. We have to look for other ways of making contact with people. At our last 'Churches Together' AGM the topic was 'Industrial Mission'; now this has always interested me. I think that the Church needs to have a much greater presence in places of work.

I have always had a great love of the theatre (we had many in Limerick when I was growing up) and I was very pleased when the Catholic Stage Guild invited me, a couple of years ago, to be the first Catholic chaplain to the National Theatre in London. The management were cooperative and gave me a staff card. There are 700 employees on the monthly payroll and maybe another 100 on special projects. It has been very fruitful. Apart from the occasional service that I am asked to provide – for example, for someone who committed suicide – I have had more people ask to speak to me and ask for prayer than I have ever had in any parish.

After the Second Vatican Council the removal of the altar rails was, for me, a very potent symbol of the removal of the barrier between clergy and laity. I feel that the Church, which I love, is too often seen as just another institutional authority, the expectations of which our lapsed people find difficulty in trying to meet. I see the Church as being too clerical in many ways – including its dress and titles! I sometimes say to priest friends, 'we are children of the Light proclaiming the Good News, but we go around in the black of mourning!'

A time of particular growth and enrichment to me was the experiment of living 'integrated into the community' in Thamesmead. Living in my one-bedroom flat helped me to be a full-time priest, with no 'property manager' responsibilities. My parish priest there encouraged me to attend different courses, and the ecumenical team ministry was a very valuable experience. My ecumenical contacts are much valued, and I have stayed over the years in a number of Anglican rectories.

I've had my low points but I praise God for the wonderful gift of the priesthood and for those who have sustained and are still sustaining me in it. I much like a prayer in the Roman Missal which asks 'that I may be an ardent but gentle servant of the Gospel'.

In September 2002 it was announced that St Patrick's College, Thurles, in County Tiperary was to close. The college had received only one enquiry about enrolment that year. It was Ireland's oldest seminary. In 1970 more than 160 men were ordained for the priesthood in Ireland; in 2001 the number was 30.

The Observer 1/9/2002

IV
Deceased members

Stephen Hinde

29 January 1937 – 24 January 1984

Stephen was born in London and baptised at St Martin-in-the-Fields, Trafalgar Square, as his parents, Michael and Elizabeth were practising Anglicans. His father worked at the Bank of England and his mother was an artist and teacher. Because of the wartime conditions the family moved to Burgess Hill, Sussex, in 1939. Soon afterwards his parents were received into the Catholic Church and Stephen, together with his elder sister Clemency, were conditionally baptised as Catholics.

Stephen went to the school at the Franciscan Convent, Burgess Hill, but had to spend some time in a sanatorium when he was seven, because he had contracted TB. His sister, Clemency, remembers this as a very unhappy time for him, as he was unkindly treated at the sanatorium, but he did not complain. He eventually returned home to be nursed there. His secondary education was at the Xaverian College, Mayfield, Sussex (quite close to the Junior Seminary of St Joseph's, Mark Cross).

Stephen was the second child of five in a very happy family. From an early age he was obsessed with cricket and spent hours playing against a wall in the back garden. His sisters were roped in to play 'Test Matches'; they were always 'Australia' and Stephen was 'England' – the latter always won! His love of cricket ran like a seam through his life. Clemency tells of how, just hours before he died, Stephen sent her down to the hospital entrance to buy a newspaper, to check the Test score from Australia, because Stephen believed that Clemency had the score wrong! He was himself a good batsman playing for local teams and later for the 'Bishop of Chichester's Ecumenical XI'.

'Perhaps because our parents were converts,' Clemency says, 'there was a good deal of overt "religion" in our childhood. This was never oppressive, but we had the Faith naturally bound into everyday life and the family played a full part in parish life.' The local clergy were frequent visitors to the Hinde home and the children of the family regularly played 'churches' – Stephen 'said Mass' and heard his sisters' confessions. 'We made up incredible sins, the meaning of which we had no idea, although we had found them mentioned in the catechism,' Clemency recalls.

From an early age Stephen had declared that he wanted to be a priest. So his family were surprised when he announced, on leaving school, that he would be 'articled' to his uncle's solicitor's firm. However, after a year, he gave this up and went to Osterley, West London, for pre-seminary preparation and training. After a year he went on to Wonersh.

After Ordination Stephen studied at the Gregorian University, Rome and gained a licentiate in Canon Law. He was then appointed to be assistant priest at Arundel Cathedral, while he taught Canon Law and Moral Theology at Wonersh. In the summer of 1968, when the birth control crisis hit the Church, Stephen felt conscience-bound to sign the letter of loyal dissent to *The Times*, along with others of his Class. In October 1968 he was permitted to go to Bristol University, where he gained an MA. On his return to the Diocese of Arundel and Brighton he was appointed to St John's, Horsham, as assistant to Fr Gregory Williams. There, his pastoral and educational skills, particularly in adult education, were much in demand.

It was at this time that his courage, as he coped with his health problems, won the hearts of people, and that their support won his gratitude. From 1976 his life reflected so many of the qualities of his admired Saint Thomas More. With compassion and integrity he exercised his office as Vice-Officialis of the Diocesan Matrimonial Tribunal, at a time when there was a major expansion in the workload. Stephen also assisted with the Westminster Archdiocese Tribunal. As the Diocesan Coordinator for the National Pastoral Congress (to be held in Liverpool) he was hopeful for the future, playing his part in the Small Groups Programme. He worked on the preparation plans from 1978 to 1980.

In 1981 major surgery became necessary and he proved a great example of patience and courage in suffering to all who knew him.

His funeral Mass was conducted by Bishop Cormac Murphy O'Connor at Arundel Cathedral, in the presence of 200 of his brother priests. He is buried at Clayton parish church, under the South Downs, near the grave of his mother, who had died two years before.

Stephen's sister, Clemency, writes of his health problems:

Stephen was incredibly plucky over the years as he coped with his illnesses. As a result of a slow growing brain tumour he was under heavy medication for epilepsy, which was a great burden, but he literally, at times, dragged himself through days. Many people never knew that he suffered this. Later, in his last illness, he exhibited extraordinary courage, hope and fight. He was both frightened and yet intensely interested in his state. Above all he had an overwhelming faith in the resurrection; in life fully lived for as long as it is given. He rarely lost his wonderful sense of fun and joy in the little things of life and in his friends and family with all their quirks, which always amused him.

The courage of a dying priest

Father Stephen Hinde knew he was dying of cancer when he was admitted to the Royal Sussex County Hospital, Brighton, but every day he visited other patients for a cheery chat. Said a spokesman at the hospital: 'He was a very brave man. He helped the sick and the nurses to cope. When he had hardly enough strength to support himself, he was still trying to help others. Everyone is very upset by his death. Everyone from the tea lady to the consultant had a great regard for him.'   *Evening Argus, 26 January 1984*

Kenneth Snaith

1 April 1923 – 12 July 1991

Kenneth was a convert and a late vocation, having worked as a sheep farmer in the Falklands before offering himself for the priesthood. Being the eldest of the Class, Ken was affectionately nicknamed 'Uncle'; this distinguished 'Uncle Ken' from Ken Bell, who was also a 'late' vocation, but younger. Born in Edinburgh on 1 April 1923, when his family moved south he went to school at Aldenham, Herts. Before going to St John's Seminary, Wonersh, he spent some time at Walworth, where provision was made, in those days, for pre-seminary training. During the last year of the seminary course he was the Dean of Students.

Kenneth's first appointment was St Boniface's Parish, Tooting, SW London. In 1967 he was appointed to the Diocesan Travelling Mission, which travelled around the many small villages of rural Kent, providing Sunday Mass and pastoral care.

During a very difficult period of change at Wonersh, Ken served as Procurator (bursar) from September 1974 until March 1975, when he was compelled to take sick leave; this lasted until October 1976.

The next appointment was to West Malling, Kent, as parish priest; but unfortunately there was another period of sick leave, from January 1977 until March of that year. Kenneth returned to be parish priest of Broadstairs, Kent. In April of 1978 he was moved to the small parish of Hersden, near Sturry, Kent. He died on 12 July 1991.

John Medcalf

31 March 1935 – 8 July 2002

At the time of the interview for this piece John was the parish priest of Redhill, Surrey. Shortly afterwards he was appointed to St Leonards, Sussex. However within weeks he was requesting leave to go to New York to work among the poor of the Bronx. He died in his sleep on 8 July 2002 while in Spain.

One of the highlights of my early priesthood, just two years after ordination, was putting my mother on the back of my motorbike and taking her to Aylesford Priory, in Kent. She was received into the Catholic Church there and I was delighted to be the one who baptised her. (We wouldn't do that today, but in those days Anglicans who became Catholics had to be conditionally baptised, at the time of reception.) I am a man of Kent, or is it a Kentish man? Canterbury was my hometown – I was born and brought up there – although my father was from Rochester. My whole family were Church of England. I went to Rochester Mathematical School and then we moved to London, because my father's job took him there. While doing National Service, in the Royal Corps of Signals, I was stationed in Austria and became a Catholic; the result, I suppose, of living in a Catholic country. Leaving the Forces at the age of 20, I was fully equipped with the skills of a wireless operator; skills that I have never used since!

I declared that I wanted to be a priest, but as I was too old to go to a Junior Seminary I was sent to the Jesuit-run College at Osterley, to prepare for the course at the Senior Seminary. Another reason for going to Osterley was that it was thought that I had not been a Catholic long enough to be sure of a vocation to the priesthood. Anyway, after six months at Osterley the Southwark Diocese accepted me.

In September 1957 I went to Wonersh, where our Year all met up. Some readers will find this hard to believe, but at that time I was very much a conformist and I accepted the disciplined training with no problem; I really wanted, very much, to be a priest and this was the established method. The way of life was the necessary price to pay, and six years of it! I wasn't critical at the time, because we had nothing else to compare it to. However, in the last couple of years, along with everyone else, I kicked at the traces. I hated that area of Surrey, because it was so pretentiously middle-class; but in fairness, at the seminary, we had little contact with it.

I have no formal degree, but I've always tried to keep up reading and study, off and on. If you limit the preparation for the priesthood to seminary training, then I wasn't well prepared, but I would include, in my preparation, the influence of my family. I enjoyed being part of it – the eldest of six children. They were all good, hard-working people and I really count that influence as an important part of my preparation. Practically all of them became Catholics. I had been ordained about two years, when I baptised my own mother.

My first appointment was to St Joseph's, Brighton. A good appointment; I thoroughly enjoyed my time there. I got on well with the parish priest, Father Patrick Leahy. He was a man of his time, but he gave me a lot of leeway, and let me get on with things. He allowed me to organise house groups to build up community in the parish. I could do anything, as long as it was not to do with organising the money!

This was the time when the diocese of Southwark was split into two: Arundel and Brighton was split away from Southwark and given its own bishop. So my bishop changed, not that I had any contact with either of them. For me 'authority' meant the parish priest and I had a good working relationship with him. It was a big parish and there were several curates, which was the way of things, at that time, and we all got on very well together. As I settled into pastoral work I began to realise that we hadn't been prepared very well for different aspects of the work and life. But I was quite cushioned from any real problems, because I had a good relationship with the other curates and we did a lot of things together. Actually I'm still in contact with three of them.

I really welcomed everything that came from the Second Vatican Council. Even before it began, I was chairman of the Liturgy Society in the Seminary. We were thought quite odd in those days for thinking that the Mass might one day be in English and for promoting the Vernacular Society. At St Joseph's we were one of the first parishes to have Mass facing the people; certainly the first in the Brighton and Hove area. The parish priest gave me permission to have a wooden altar specially made. And right from the beginning the people appreciated the change. There is no doubt the liturgy improved immensely as a result of the changes.

Really speaking, most of my experience of the application of the decrees of the Vatican Council has been overseas and there is no doubt that there would have been no liberation theology, a non-European theology, without the laity.

After five years in Brighton I volunteered for Peru. The idea had been growing inside me. Then, one day, we had a letter from the bishop, Bishop Cashman, telling us that the Vatican was encouraging European priests to volunteer for Latin America and he invited anyone interested to apply. I wrote back immediately, by return of post! We did not go with the Society of St James, which organised many of the priest volunteers, but with the Columban Fathers. They organised everything. I went out in February 1968 and found that there was a four-month training course, which covered everything, not just the language.

I had a real shock when I was sent to a shantytown parish, just outside Lima, called El Monton (that was the nickname, it means 'the garbage mountain', and the whole parish was indeed not much more than that mountain of garbage). Life was made a little easier by being in a team of three priests, with whom I gelled very well. One was an Australian, one was Irish and then there was me, the Englishman! It was a very poor parish; three of us slept in one dingy room. I was only there for a year, because I got hepatitis and the Columbans shipped me out to the States to be sorted out. I was the first Columban ever to get it – we were classed as associate Columbans – and they looked after me well.

After a few months, I returned to Lima and I was given another parish in the shantytown. We lived with the people and were there to serve them. The next thing was the rural libraries. Three of us, all Englishmen, decided that we wanted to return to being diocesan priests, without the umbrella of the Religious Society, the Columban Fathers. We wanted to work directly with the local bishop, and we wanted to treat the problem of poverty at its roots. One priest went south and two of us went north to the mountainous areas. I went to the northern Andes to Cajamarca, determined not to be there on my own as a priest; so three of us linked up to form a team, and we worked together. One was an Englishman, from the Westminster diocese, Michael Garnett, who is still out there, and writes occasionally for *The Tablet*. The other was Rudi Eichenlant, a German priest. He has since returned to Germany and married. We each had dozens of villages to look after.

The rural libraries started when a young lad, Leonardo Herrera, came knocking at my door. He wanted to see 'books', which he'd never seen before. I said, 'But surely if you read and write you must have seen "books"'. 'No', he said, 'we cut a large cactus leaf with a machete every Monday and with a nail or a key we carve the letters and numbers on the leaf, to learn.' Then I showed him a book and he took it and gingerly held it and smelt it. It took him several minutes to work out how it worked. It was a history of Peru and he went away clutching it. I told him that I would lend it to him for two weeks. That night I thought out how I could set up libraries in the villages and get some funding. It was late and I was just dropping off to sleep when there was loud knocking at the door and it was Leonardo back again! He'd come down from his village; he'd finished the book and he was triumphant. 'You can't have read it,' I said. 'You have no electricity'. 'I have read it,' he said. 'I borrowed some candles from your church!' He'd been up all night reading the book. This year (2001) is the thirtieth anniversary of the setting up of the rural libraries. There are now just over 600 of them through the Andes villages. Using special colourfully woven saddlebags, either over the backs of donkeys or over their own shoulders, people take the books from village to village. They get ten books in one side of the saddlebags and ten books in the other. Sometimes it's a two-day journey. In my time we bought the books to distribute them, but my successor developed the important stage of producing their own rural library books. While I ministered to the people, this was my work for ten years. Much of the time, the authorities were not too happy, because encouraging the poor to read is viewed as a subversive activity. A mayor of a local town said, 'Why don't you get funds for a television set for each village instead. That wouldn't disturb anyone or anything.' Nor, of course, would they learn anything. The wonderful thing now is that the people themselves are writing the books, which are distributed. So they are reading their own publications. My Peruvian successor got death threats and spent time in jail. He was denounced and the libraries were denounced; that would have been in 1984. Actually there was a recent full-page article in a Sunday supplement of an Italian popular daily reporting and celebrating the 30th anniversary.

After 15 years in Peru, in 1982, I came back to England and worked for a year in Brixton, to give me a period of adjustment. From there I went to Hindhead. After a while I received an invitation – which I accepted – from literacy groups in Nicaragua. The Minister of Education was a Jesuit and the Minister of Culture was Father Ernesto Cardinal and they wanted post-literacy projects and some kind of library service. And I had a parish to care for. Actually for most of my life I've only been a weekend priest!

I was three years in Nicaragua and had firsthand experience of the battles that took place between the local people and the US-backed Contras. Those experiences were published in *Letters From Nicaragua* published by CIIR (see the three extracts from *Letters from Nicaragua* on pages 119-121).

I returned to England and had four very happy years in Shoreham-by-Sea, but still kept in regular contact with Latin America. After that appointment I returned to Latin America and went to El Salvador for five years, where I was deputy editor of the Archdiocesan weekly newspaper. It was 1992 and I arrived soon after the peace accord had been signed between the insurgents and the government. Life was very tense and there was a lot of poverty. In 1997 I returned to England and spent an interesting year at the Missionary Institute at Mill Hill, going around parishes and schools giving talks on Latin America. Being at the Institute also provided me with the opportunity to keep in touch with developments out there. My heart's half here and half over there; I'm a bigamist really!

Yes, there were low spots and particularly when I first went abroad. In those early years in Peru I immersed myself completely in the life and culture. I cut myself off from everything English; I didn't want to hear any news from England or receive newspapers, magazines or books in English. I found this was a necessary stage to go through. For ten years I became Peruvian; it was a survival tactic. A lot of Europeans remained in regular touch, keeping alive their allegiance to a football team at home, following all the scores, and all that, but I couldn't.

For two years, from 1978 to 1980, I gave up the Church and the priesthood; not the education work. It was at Cajamarca, while I was working on the rural libraries project. I didn't function as a priest for those two years; the bishop was extremely good. I fell in love with a colleague, who was chaplain of the university with me, but it was unrequited. However it was basically more than that. There was the whole question of the grinding poverty that I witnessed all around me every day. The whole thing didn't seem to be going anywhere. A lot of us could not see where it was all going; what sort of God could it be that allowed the majority of the human race to live in such awful conditions. The Church was marvellous compared to the State, but it seemed to be slow to respond and I just felt that I couldn't carry on celebrating. So for about two years I didn't celebrate the Eucharist. A lot of priests just gave up, they could not cope with the situation; a lot got married. It was an important chapter in the history of the Church in the twentieth century: the massive migration of priests, sisters and then later on, lay people throughout Latin America.

It was the poor who brought me back. The readers at the

libraries wanted Mass, as well as books. They brought me back and restored my faith. We missionaries had a phrase that we used: 'It's the poor who evangelise us.' It was really a two-way process; we helped to make them articulate, then they brought reality to us.

What, looking back over 40 years, would I have changed? Well, its all hypothetical isn't it? I'm not particularly good at looking back. There were so many things that I had to teach myself; for example, I had to study Marxism on my own. It was the Cold War period and the temptation was constantly there to look for left-wing solutions in Latin America; you really had to understand Marxism. You had to understand why it was that ordinary people just loved leaders like Che Guevara and Fidel Castro. Fortunately in Peru we had a lot of good theologians, of whom the best known is Gustavo Gutiérrez. They challenged us to be involved in ongoing formation and study. I certainly wish that we had not had that unbroken period of six years of seminary training. I would like to see seminarians doing two or three years in England, then if they have to do six years, part of the rest should be overseas; perhaps a year in Spain or Italy, then the rest out in Asia, Africa or Latin America.

People 'left' our Class of '63 in different ways. There was the really sad 'leaving' of Ken Bell and Joe Ware, through their accidents. Then dear Stephen Hinde died of a brain tumour in 1984. It was also sad that I didn't maintain contact with them, but that was partly because I was out of the country. I would like to know what happened to Sean O'Callaghan, Dave Payne and Mike Ivers; I hope they are happy. It would be wonderful and comforting to know that they are happy and have had fulfilling lives.

Looking back over 40 years of ministry I take most pride in the Rural Library Project. I laid the foundations; when I left, there were about 300 and it has continued to develop to over 600. It's essentially a qualitative growth. It has been calculated that there are 50,000 readers a year using the libraries. From a long-term point of view this must be preparing generations to be able to direct their own lives.

If I was invited back to Wonersh to speak to this year's candidates for the priesthood I would say, 'realise the catholicity of yourselves. Go and experience other cultures. Have a few months, perhaps a year, sharing and experiencing life outside your own culture. I left the Anglican Church because they were not 'catholic' enough. We need to experience the catholicity of the Church. Pope John XXIII said we should recognise the signs of the times, but we really need to recognise the signs of the places, too.

Before we talk about developments in the ministry, my priority would be to decentralise the Church. What is suitable to Africa is not suitable to Europe. We have got to have Patriarchs of Latin America, Asia and Africa, so that they can say, in one continent, our society and culture need, for example, women priests, but you, in your setting, don't need them. It could be 200 years before the need might arise in that particular society.

I would like to see, in our cultural setting, the Ordained ministry developing by the acceptance of women priests. We are just going to have to tackle that. The Anglican experiment is invaluable. I would like to see, for men and for women, a division between the secular ministry, where celibacy would be optional, and the Religious Orders, which would carry on the tradition of celibacy. I think that's the way we have to go forward.

From a private letter to the editor from John, dated 13th July 1993

My celebration of our 30th was almost as solitary as yours; I had the company of two Scots: a priest called Tim and a bottle called Johnny Walker! . . . perhaps we are all doomed to have our life journeys better appraised by others than by ourselves, to have others see the sense of our friction, where we can often only see senseless and wasteful conflict. Every part of our lives needs its own spirituality I suppose, and perhaps we are all grappling with what I call 'paternity' at the moment . . . i.e. allowing a younger generation of people to share in our experience and even our wisdom, and enabling them to do what we would like to do, had we their energy, but having the humility to let them do it in a way we would probably disapprove of. I am finding this stage very difficult.

Let us all continue to pray for each other . . . it will be so great to meet up merrily in heaven, with Stephen Hinde and 'Uncle' Ken Snaith. Eventually with Sean O'C and David Payne and others who have fallen out of Class contact, but whose pilgrimages are also so precious. Not forgetting our two physical invalids. It takes a lot of faith at times to see God's loving hands in all this mishmash of our lives, and our influence on each other.

Three extracts from John Medcalf's *Letters from Nicaragua*

Parroquia Cristo Redentor
Muelle de los Bueyes
Nicaragua
29th July 1986
Dear Friends

Thank God Nicaraguans have a sense of humour. A few weeks ago I was travelling on horseback through some of the worst mud swamp-lands in this rural parish. Perhaps a herd of African hippopotomi might, within a few generations, have adapted to the ubiquitous mud! I rode (rather plunged) past an extraordinary mêlée of timber that must have been the farmhouse and noticed the farmer had painted boldly across the doorway the name of his farm; 'Better than nothing'.
. . . In my weaker moments I am tempted to organise soup kitchens. Many priests do that sort of thing in different parts of the world. Certain readers of these letters might then be relieved that I had stopped 'being political'. But I know this would be wrong. The problem in Nicaragua *is* political, caused by political interference from the most powerful country in the world. If the whole of the Central American region were allowed to choose its own political future, without hindrance and pressures, these people would be among the best fed in the world. I intend therefore to stand by these Nicaraguan farm-workers, and to make known the justice of their cause. My God is not a Lord of Death and War, nor a Defender of the 'status quo' in a world where the status of $^2/_3$ of the people is inhuman. I feel sure that life for these people is meant to be a *lot* better than nothing. God bless you.

Padre Juan Luis (Medcalf)

119

12th December 1986

Dear Friends

The greater part of this parish is a political no man's land. Once I leave the heavily-guarded highroad uniting the Atlantic and Pacific oceans, it is as if I had entered a different country. This vast hinterland is divided into 'comarcas' or regions. We have over fifty in our parish and I recently spent a lot of time visiting them on horseback. A typical 'comarca' would have thirty or forty farmsteads with at least a kilometre of rough muddy track between each wooden hut. The only public building would be the Catholic chapel.

The Delegate of the Word of God in Las Pavas (meaning 'The Turkey hens') gave me a great welcome to his community on November 13th. 45-year-old Zacarias Garzon had persuaded almost every family to attend the 24-hour Mission I was to direct in the chapel, that had formerly served as a school until the 'Contras' abducted the teacher. He introduced me as the only 'sacredote ingles' working in Nicaragua, and jocularly reminded his fellow farmers that most of the Englishmen who had visited the Caribbean in the past had been pirates looking for Spanish gold. In my reply I thanked Zacarias on behalf of all turkey-eating Britons, for Central America's gift to the world, and suggested that the turkeys after which their village had been named had brought more pleasure to Britain than the Spanish gold. There followed many hours of baptisms, weddings, confessions, first communions and question-and-answer sermons.

Three weeks later, on December 2, the Contras dragged Zacarias Garzon from his hut and slit his throat in the nearby forest. Why Zacarias? He was not known to be a Sandinista supporter. I know that he was prepared for death. Those who knew him will treasure the memory of a courageous leader. He joins a long roll of heroes and martyrs in Central America's struggle for independence and dignity.

Padre Juan Luis

March 16th 1987

Dear Friends

March is 'back-to-school' month in Nicaragua. We have 62 schools in our rural parish, but this year only 40 are functioning. The others – in remote villages, populated by maize-growing farmers – are closed because the Contras have murdered the teachers.

I have spent a good part of the month visiting the schools that remain open. The children are remarkably resilient, even those who have witnessed rape, torture and assassination. They and their teachers expect me to lead prayers for the dead, say Mass for the end of hostilities, and give encouragement and hope . . .

We inaugurated our first Rural Library on Sunday, in Cara de Mono. You will remember that this village was the scenario of a Contra attack on November 24th last year, days after my arrival in the parish. The Library is named after Ivan Torres, the 17-year-old killed in the battle.

I had very little time for sleep in Holy Week. In Nicaragua shops, offices and schools close for the entire week, and not just for two days. The people spilled onto the streets for multitudinous processions on Palm Sunday, complete with real donkeys and real palms. Men and women alternated to carry an exaggeratedly heavy wooden cross through the villages on Good Friday. On Holy Saturday traditional bonfires blazed for hours outside the churches in the darkness that precedes the dawn of Easter. Sermons, I felt, were superfluous: these people know more about death and hope and living Christianity than their shepherd who walks with them.

Devotedly, Padre Juan Luis

V
Out of the active ministry

Sean O'Callaghan

Sean was last known to be living in Dublin, Ireland

After Ordination Sean's first appointment was to the parish of Our Lady, Star of the Sea, Crooms Hill, Greenwich, SE London. He was the first member of the Year to leave the active ministry, and that was about 1967.

Sean and his wife went back to Dublin, from where his family originated, and he worked in the construction industry. His wife died some years ago. Nothing further is known, as Sean does not appear to have kept in touch with anyone.

Michael Ivers

Michael was last known to be living in the Brisbane area of Australia

Michael was educated by the Xaverians at Clapham College and was always an active sportsman, both there and at Wonersh. He took a full and practical part in all the seminary's social events; for example, building scenery for plays and the Gilbert and Sullivan productions. As the photograph on page 140 reveals, he enjoyed a stage role too.

After Ordination Michael's first appointment was to St Joseph's parish, Roehampton, where he found himself with Kevin Pelham in a newly constituted parish. After two and half years he was appointed to the Catholic Children's Society as secretary. Michael, very much the practical man, was not comfortable with being tied to an office desk, and after a while, asked to be returned to parish life. He was sent to be an assistant to Father Ken Allan, a well-known liberal parish priest of St Aidan's, Coulsdon, Surrey.

There was great upheaval in that parish with the crisis in the Church over the *Humanae Vitae* encyclical and the public departure of the parish priest to marry. Michael signed *The Times* letter of loyal dissent (with two others from his Year) and appears to have left the active ministry not long afterwards.

Michael married Carol, a teacher, and they had two children; a boy and a girl. They appear to have lived in Somerset at this time and Michael ran an antiques restoration workshop. His wife took the two children to Australia and, after some time, Michael followed. It is believed that his marriage broke up some time after this. He stayed in the Perth area, to be close to his children, and worked as a motor mechanic.

After some time Michael married again; an Australian named Lesley. They moved south of Perth to Pemberton, where they worked together on a tourist centre/safari complex.

In the 90s Michael moved across to Brisbane, on the other side of Australia. His present whereabouts are unknown to his friends in England.

David Payne

David is a retired teacher living in South West London

After his ordination David went on to further study at St Edmund's House, Oxford. He signed the letter of loyal dissent to *The Times* (see the Introduction) in 1968 and left the active ministry not long afterwards. He taught for many years and is now retired, living in SW London. David is remembered with affection and respect by his confrères, but he was not comfortable with contributing to this 'celebration'.

James Wilson

Jim Wilson is presently an Independent Financial Adviser

I originate from Surbiton, 'the epitome of suburbia'! Born in 1936, I am the eldest of five. My mother was a convert; becoming a Catholic when my parents married. Both of them were children of large families. At four I started school at the Manor House Convent School, Surbiton. Even then I was taller than most and teachers always thought I was older and should be doing better at school. I transferred from there to the Donhead Lodge Prep School – the prep part of Wimbledon College. Fees were about £25 a term in those days, but my family was never very well off and it was an awful struggle for them to find the money. I took the 11+ a year early and was at Wimbledon College from 1947 to 1954. I achieved O-Levels in Maths (elementary!), English Language and Literature, and French (a year late because of my birth date) and then A-Levels in Latin, Greek, and Ancient History, plus the Scholarship General paper. When I left at 18 I was waiting to do National Service, so in the meantime I worked in the Education Department at County Hall, Kingston-upon-Thames. My father worked in the same building, in the motor taxation department. That experience helped me to decide that I definitely didn't want to work in local government!

In January 1955 I went into the Royal Air Force. I did my basic training at RAF Hednesford and we had to camp out on Cannock Chase in a snowy April. I went home on leave that Easter feeling quite ill. The parish priest, who was relying on me to help organise the Holy Week services, was disappointed because I spent much of the time in bed. When I went back to camp I had to report sick with swollen ankles. I was hobbling around so much that the other aircraftmen hummed the Death March from Saul as I went past the canteen queue! I ended up in an ambulance off to RAF Hospital Wroughton with rheumatic fever. I spent six weeks there. Afterwards I convalesced at RAF Chessington, close to home (and the Zoo!). I then returned to RAF Locking to complete my training as a wireless mechanic. I wanted to learn Russian, because I have a facility with languages, but they laughed at that idea and sent me to tinker with transformers and transmitters. I finished my time in the RAF installing instrument landing systems for bombers. I was very lucky; we went round from camp to camp and virtually worked our own hours.

When I came out I had to make up my mind what to do. I'd been to daily Mass as a boy – in fact my father had said that although we were hard up, he'd rather have me going to Mass each morning than have a morning paper round – and continued, whenever I could, in the RAF. I wanted to work with and serve people, so I offered myself for the priesthood, but I had no desire whatever to go to the Junior Seminary at Mark Cross. There wasn't much fear of that, though, because by now I was 21, and already had Latin and Greek.

At Wonersh, for the first term, I had to attend Jim McConnon's dreaded Latin classes, but soon got out of them. After the RAF the discipline of the seminary was no problem; it was the petty little rules that irritated. Rules like you couldn't step inside another's room and were forbidden to talk to anyone in the toilets. I could understand the reasons for some of the rules, but they struck me as unnecessary and outdated. A lot of the rules were to stop friendships blossoming and becoming 'particular' and exclusive; a precaution that was only necessary because of the restricted atmosphere. The business of being locked up from September to 27 December and then again from January to July was nonsense. Personally it would have been so much better for my family if I'd gone home for the family day we were granted on Easter Monday. My father could ill afford to bring the whole family to see me. Even though the diocese funded my training, without which support I could not have contemplated the course, keeping me in pocket money for six years at Wonersh involved a big sacrifice for my father, when he could have had me, as the eldest of a fairly large family, out in the world earning money to help out.

Regarding the seminary course itself, I believe that the content of the Philosophy and Theology, for the purposes of work in a parish setting, was unnecessarily detailed. But it was the isolation, being kept from the outside world, which was the most harmful. The community atmosphere was a hothouse one; a glorified boarding school. It didn't prepare you for life in an average parish. I was just so glad, by the time I had finished, that I had those two maturing years in the Air Force. That experience gave me a better understanding of people and relationships than the seminary course. I witnessed in parishes later, in the way clergy spoke about people and events when they got together, the boarding-school mentality that they had picked up at Mark Cross and Wonersh.

Of course there were highlights and happy times at Wonersh. I remember how I helped to produce *Merrie England* and I particularly enjoyed looking after the garden I had there. A good time was had, but in a boarding-school fashion.

My first appointment was to St Mary's, Preston Park, Brighton. George Tinker was the other curate and Ted Fooks was the parish priest. He was a real thinker; he'd got people involved and he'd anticipated a lot of the changes that were coming in the liturgy. He was truly forward-looking and took me with him to Worth Abbey for their well-regarded Worth Conferences. They were excellent and I got a lot out of them. I enjoyed Preston Park and still have friends there whom I've kept in touch with ever since. The presbytery has been rebuilt and there have been some other changes, but I always feel at home when I go down there. I was in that parish for five years.

One morning a letter arrived telling me that I had been appointed to Farnham. That was a pleasant enough experience. I got on very well with Father Hugh Raynham, who was a delightful character. Actually when I left there I used to go down, on my days off, with my mother, to visit him in his retirement. I can only remember one problem in that parish. For some reason that I could never fathom I didn't get on with the headteacher of the parish primary school. He didn't like me going into the school, although it was right next door to the parish church. The church, priests' house and school are all on the same site. The children used to come through the church car park and I'd go out to talk to them; but the head teacher did not like that. We ended up with only Father Raynham going into the school. After five happy years at Farnham I was sent to Epsom.

Epsom was a parish with numerous hospitals; a general hospital, a cottage hospital and four or five mental or psychiatric hospitals. Willie Westlake, who was the parish priest, would ask when you came in for lunch, 'Have you done your hospitals?' The hospitals were shared out among the three curates. (It was at this time that my father died.) I'd been there four and half years, and the work in the psychiatric wards, with disturbed and mentally ill people, was beginning to get me down. I remember well a meeting of all the chaplains, at one of the hospitals. One chaplain asked the question that had been in my head, 'Who cares for the carers?' Those words really struck a chord in me. As far as I was concerned that was the best thing to come out of that meeting. Constantly, it seemed to me, no one cared for us or about us; not even the parish priest.

So after four and half years we had a parish visitation. The bishop came for the weekend and went through all the Masses, and we took him by arrangement to see some of the sick. I suggested to him that it was about time I had a move. He replied, 'Who'd want you for a curate for just 18 months?' – implying that after that period of time I'd be given my own parish. So I thought, I'll settle back and wait; it took another three years! So I was seven and a half years in the Epsom parish. Then I was sent to follow Tim Jelf at the Holy Angels, Ash, Surrey. It proved to be a lovely parish. There was a well-organised parish council and the parishioners even got together while I was there and decorated the church. Before I formally arrived I went down a couple of times and Tim and I concelebrated the Mass together. I told the people, 'Don't forget he's Tim and I'm Jim. If things change at all it's because he's Tim and I'm Jim'. And we all got on famously.

The disillusionment, however, did not go away. I began to find it difficult to pray for my bishop, with whom I was utterly disillusioned. He had made a recent visitation to my parish, but had showed little real interest in my work, coming across instead as aloof and uncaring. I couldn't help feeling that if my work meant so little to him there was little point in continuing.

I remember having a chat with my mother and asking her how she would feel if I pulled out. She said, 'I know you have been unhappy with things for a long time. If that is what you want to do, do it.' She had quite a lot to put up with, at that time, because there were other problems in the family for her to worry about. She was always hugely supportive to me and I'd come home on my day off and celebrate Mass with her, using the table in her living room.

It was at this time, when I was struggling with disillusionment, that I met Mary. After I decided that I was going to leave, our relationship grew and I introduced her to my mother. I certainly did not leave to get married; I left because I was fed-up and disillusioned. I was fed-up with belonging to everyone and, at the same time, belonging to no one. As a priest you always have to be smiling, always ready to listen to people. The disillusionment had gradually crept up on me and I reached the point where I didn't want to pray for the pope or my bishop. When I had to go into hospital to have my hernia repaired, for the second time, I told Bishop Cormac that when I left hospital I was not going to return to the parish. He said, 'We'd better have a chat.' When we met, I told him how I felt neglected and sidelined; he responded with 'mea culpa', but it was too little too late. There were other things that I complained about; for example, favouritism shown to Roman-trained clergy, who just turned up in the diocese from Rome and were given prestigious jobs.

My aunt had died the previous year and left my mother a small bungalow down in the New Forest. Mum wanted to go and see my sister in New Zealand and decided to use the money from the sale of the bungalow for that purpose. After the operation, and while I was convalescing I worked out a round-the-world trip, taking three months, for the two of us. We went off to Singapore, Bangkok, Hong Kong and Honolulu; then on to Auckland, for three weeks with my sister. It was 1982 and we watched the Falklands Task Force sailing from Britain on Hong Kong television. Then we travelled on to Los Angeles, up to Calgary, by coach to Vancouver and then on to spend a few weeks with my sister in Kingston; and finally home.

On my return from the globetrotting, I went up to where I am living now; on £13-a-week unemployment benefit. Mary and I had found the house, belonging to a charity that ran almshouses, before I set off on the round-the-world tour. Mary had an acquaintance in that area, from a time before she got married when she had been a nanny. We were offered the licence to occupy the property and Mary moved up there in the April. I joined her in the May, after I returned. We were very hard up. Mary received a little income from helping to run a playgroup in the village and I had the unemployment benefit. I kept applying for jobs, but the nearest I got to a proper job was acting as an unqualified care assistant, on £69 a week. Apart from my A-Levels I had no qualifications. I remained unemployed for six months, until I got a job with a Natural Herbal Skin Care firm. While working for them I came across a man working for Canada Life Insurance; he told me what good employers they were and that they were recruiting at that time. On interview, I found that I liked the company and they seemed to like me. I was working on commission and the business gradually built up. I was with them until October last year, when they sacked us all! Since then I have been freelance in the life insurance business. I sometimes joke that in my previous 'life' I was providing fire insurance, now I sell life insurance!

Mary and I were married in Oundle. Shortly afterwards, I decided that I just had to get more money coming in, because we couldn't afford to run the central heating and had a new baby due! We could only afford one bag of Coalite for the Rayburn in the kitchen, once a week; and we endured some really hard winters in the early days. But the Lord has been very good to us over the years. Since I began to earn better money we have been able to sort out lots of things and even afford some good holidays for the children. We are still in the same house, which we rent from this charity. They have been very good to us and in the last few years have done a lot of belated refurbishment of the property. My mother found her flat in Epsom was getting too expensive after she retired from the Inland Revenue at 68, so she came to live in a bungalow close to us.

I've always been open with each of the parish priests we have had, and left it to him if he wanted to use me in the parish. One of them got me to do the parish accounts, until I wouldn't do them his way. He was from a wealthy family, but he didn't want it known that he was using his own funds to get the parish out of debt to the diocese. I felt he should at least be credited with what he was doing, but he didn't like that, so he took the accounts back. If the parish priest wants me to read, or serve if a server doesn't turn up, I'm there to be called upon.

Alice was born in 1984, which was when I joined Canada Life. Michael came along in 1987, by which time I was reasonably well established in the insurance field. I collected titles as I progressed and ended up as an Executive Consultant. Yes, I've got my Canada Life cuff-links with my initials on! I obtained my professional qualifications from the Life Insurance Association. You have to jump through all the right hoops nowadays, as the insurance industry has become so highly regulated. Being in insurance is rather like having my own parish; I have my own people, whom I take care of. There could be 600 to 800 clients, but you can't really look after more than 250. Now that I'm independent and not attached to any particular company, I'm hoping to be even more acceptable to all and sundry.

When you are independent the paperwork is simply enormous, it can take a whole day to process one case and send it off. I enjoy the talking to people and trying to help them, but I certainly don't enjoy the paperwork.

I have no clear idea what seminary training is like these days, but I gather that it is a lot more open. Students also seem to have a greater opportunity to decide on celibacy because they are out and about, mixing more with people than we ever did. One word of advice I would dare to give to students is, always remember that the Church is not 'them up there', with their code of canon law, but 'them out here', whom you will be serving. The Church is not rules and regulations; it's the people. Very sadly the institutional Church is just not attractive or appealing to people any more. Despite our example, the three children in my family, who have passed 18, just don't go to church any more; and that is common in most Catholic families nowadays. Happily one of them will still come willingly to Mass for special occasions, like Grandma's Anniversary or Christmas and Easter. Somehow the Church needs to explain to people why they need to go to church; convince them that it is a good and necessary thing.

When our generation was growing up, Mass-going was part habit and part discipline. You got into the practice and you just did it. We have to get away from the desiccated parish priest who is set in his ways. Some of the clergy need to get down from their pedestals, and the people need to let them do this and help them to get in touch with reality. The average parish priest doesn't understand how a family ticks over: he doesn't understand the rows that go on to get teenagers out of the door and into Mass or to get them to take part in some activity in the community. So many of our clergy live in a totally different world. However, they can't be blamed, because the way things are structured they are unable to enter and be part of the real world. Even when they stop, for a few days, with brothers and sisters who have families, they are not truly experiencing the real thing. On those occasions people are on their best behaviour because uncle, the priest, is stopping. Our bishops have got to realise that their job isn't to be going to meetings but to be out among the people and their priests; giving support and encouragement. (There are surely priests who can be appointed 'vicars' to attend meetings and report back to the bishop.)

I could very well still be there, in the active ministry, if I had been valued as a person. It took me a long time to get over leaving. I felt a bit of a failure. There was that stinging comment, from Pope John Paul II, that those who took their hand from the plough were unworthy of the Lord. At the time that I left, I reasoned that no one looks down on anyone else who changes his job. Doctors, for example, who opt out and become administrators or novelists, are not looked down on or held up for public debate, so why should anyone not be able to leave the priesthood if they wish?

God has been good to me over the past 40 years. I can thank him for the 20 years in the priesthood and for the 20 years in a happy marriage. In both parts there have been ups and downs; but God has always been there for me.

Anthony Castle

Tony Castle is a retired teacher; until recently Head of RE at St Bernard's High School, Westcliff-on-Sea, Essex

My earliest memory is of a dugout, or air-raid shelter, in 'Hell Fire Corner', as the Press called Dover in 1941. I can still remember the dank, earthy smell of the place. The dugout had been in the corner of my grandfather's yard, outside his workshop, among the wagons and carts awaiting his attention. He was a wheelwright and I've always been proud of both Dover and my craftsman background.

The Catholic Faith in our family originated from France. My great grandfather had come over from Calais, settled, but not brought his family up as Catholics. About 1927, the local parish priest, Father William Law, while out visiting one day, called on my grandmother and the result was that she returned to the Faith, and my mother, who was 16 at the time, was baptised. There have been other conversions over the years; my grandfather became a Catholic, in hospital, three days before he died. My father was received into the Church in his late sixties and my wife became a Catholic, when we had been married 20 years.

After we returned to war-torn Dover from evacuation, in 1945, I went to the parish school, St Paul's, under the tender care of the Sisters of Charity. Soon after I became an altar server. Priests were regular visitors at our home and, spending time with the two young curates and admiring them, I began to think that I too would like to be a priest. In fact I cannot remember a time when I've ever wanted to be anything else. About the age of 10, I told my mother. The first reaction of my father was that I was much too young to be thinking about such a life. How could I yet understand the sacrifices involved, he asked? At 13 however, I went off to the Junior Seminary at Mark Cross, near Tunbridge Wells, on the Kent–Sussex border.

When I arrived at Mark Cross, in September 1951, I was the youngest and smallest student in the place. I remember how embarrassed I was when my parents, who did not understand the item 'house shoes' on the clothes list, sent me with rather dinky soft slippers. I had to wear them, as I had nothing else and I was immediately given the nickname 'Twinkle Toes'!

Dad was a lorry driver and my mother – as women did in those days – stayed at home and looked after the family (I am the eldest of three). We were not well off – for example, I can remember only one family holiday, and there was no car or telephone. However, despite that, I learnt many years later, that my Dad insisted on paying something, every month, towards my upkeep at Mark Cross.

Faced with 12 years away from my family – never having Christmas at home, with two holidays a year, a couple of weeks after Christmas, and eight weeks in the summer – I was determined to persevere. Daily life was very Victorian and strict, with long periods of silence and many petty rules; for example, not being allowed to carry a comb and not going up stairs two steps at a time. Apart from a half-day family visit on Easter Monday, we spent no time with our families from January to July. The 'Rule' forbade us to speak to 'externs', which meant we could not even visit a local shop. Of course, there was no television and we could only listen to the radio for 30 minutes each day, during the evening recreation. There was plenty of sport, which I enjoyed, although I was never particularly good at football, cricket or hockey.

By modern standards it was pretty grim, but I was focused on wanting to prepare well for the priesthood, however long it took, and, once settled, I was quite happy and contented.

At the end of my fifth year, many superficial changes took place in the daily life of the seminary. For example, the daily attire was changed from wearing black cassocks, with sashes and birettas to grey trousers with black blazers. Most of those who had started with me in 1951 were moved out to St John's seminary at Wonersh; leaving me as one of the eldest. The Rector, Monsignor Corbishley, appointed me as the new Head Prefect (they had been called 'wardens' before).

On arrival at Wonersh I found that life was a more mature version of Mark Cross. Instead of being 'Castle' (our Christian names were never used at the Junior Seminary) I was now 'Mr' Castle and attired, when we went out, in a black suit with accompanying trilby hat! We were only allowed out of the seminary in groups of three, and never alone or just with one other! On the social side, the annual Gilbert and Sullivan operas were fun; and so professionally produced. As a first-tenor I was usually cast in a female role; my Katisha in *The Mikado* was particularly well acclaimed! My only male part was as a pirate in *The Pirates of Penzance* (see page 140). Although never really a sportsman, I joined in all the sports, but long-distance cross-country running became my particular forte, winning the seminary 'marathon' (not the full distance) three years in succession.

The most wonderful confirmation of my belief that I had a vocation came very unexpectedly, on my 25th birthday. It was about two weeks before Ordination. A letter arrived in unfamiliar handwriting. I was alarmed at first to see that it was from my Dad, because Mum had always been the one to write, over the 12 years. He began by telling me not to panic, Mum, he reassured me, was not ill; he just had something special to share with me. 'Your big day is very close now,' he went on. 'You know we have prayed for you for a long time and I think the answer is near. Now is the time to tell you something that I haven't even told your mother. The first time that I prayed for you to become a priest was on the morning you were born. I will tell you all about it some other time.' I was deeply moved and I still have that precious letter.

I also have the retreat resolutions that I made each year; they reveal a very serious effort to prepare well for the long-awaited Ordination day. At last the great day came. My Ordination photos show me standing, in a red vestment, next to proud parents, my brother Peter, and sister Christine, and eight guests.

My first appointment was to Nunhead, which is next to Peckham Rye, in SE London. I was eager to get started and rang the parish priest, who will remain nameless, for reasons that will become apparent. He told me to take an additional three weeks holiday

Pirates of Penzance
produced by Stephen Hinde
stage sets by Michael Ivers

Pirates: C. Benyon, J. Bliss, A. Burnham, A. Castle M. Ivers, J. Pannett
Pirate apprentice (Frederic): F. Hartley   *Pirate Maid (Ruth):* K. Pelham

Policemen: K. Bell, P. Ryman, A. Ford, D. Griffith, F. Tynan,
C. Baker, D. Weston

and seemed in no hurry for me to join him. When I eventually arrived I found a very small presbytery and a small, simply adorned, church. Nora was the housekeeper and she was more welcoming than the parish priest. It soon became apparent that the parish priest wanted to be on his own, but needed me, because there were too many Sunday Masses for him to cope with. There were five morning Masses, on the hour from 8 to midday. (This was in the age of the Dialogue Mass – in Latin – and no evening Mass.) My parish priest insisted that I be present at all five Masses. We went across to the church at 7.30am and either he would celebrate the first three – at which I preached – or I would celebrate and he would preach; then we changed over for the last two Masses of the morning. This was at the time – before the changes of the Second Vatican Council – when we were fasting from midnight, so there was nothing to eat or drink until dinner at 1.30pm. It was quite tough.

Apart from a turn in the confessional box on a Saturday, I was not expected to do anything, except look after the altar servers. The parish priest kept all the other duties, like funerals, baptisms, marriage preparation, and convert instruction, to himself. I asked for a list of parishioners, so that I could go visiting, but he told me he couldn't find one! Eventually I gave up waiting and went out knocking on doors, without any list, but this did not please him. I drifted into the small parish youth club and that prompted the parish priest to ask me to take it over and develop it. He also instructed me to start a Cub Pack and a Scout Troop. I was terrified, because I had never mixed with young people, particularly girls, before, and I knew precious little about Scouts and Cubs. To cut a long story short, I did get immersed in youth work; the youth club developed and, after training as a Group Scout Leader, I founded a good size Cub Pack and Scout Troop.

However, in the house, relationships were going from bad to worse. We had our meals in a tiny dining room, which doubled as our lounge; and, despite my best efforts, there was no conversation. I couldn't work out why the atmosphere was so bad, and why the parish priest was so hostile. There were only two telephones in the house, one in his study and the other in his bedroom; I was not expected to use either, without first asking permission. Living conditions were bleak; for example, there was one poorly decorated bathroom with a basin falling off the wall, for which I found a stick to help prop it up.

The parish priest told me that there were insufficient Mass stipends for both of us (I later discovered that this was not true), so I was given £2 a week, and of course no share in any offerings coming from baptisms, funerals and so forth. Fortunately my only 'outgoings' was my monthly journey to Dover to see my parents.

The parish priest insisted on celebrating the 7.30am Mass every morning and afterwards he would mysteriously disappear; returning about 9.30am. Usually he would disappear again in the afternoon about 3pm and return about 5.30pm. A couple of times a week, he would not return to the presbytery until very late in the evening. I was delighted when that happened, because I could have a stress-free meal on my own.

One day the mystery was solved; and my life was affected forever. It was my day off, a Wednesday in November. I had been at Nunhead for about four months. Returning from a visit to Dover, I was walking up Hollydale Road from the station, at about 10.30pm on a rather wet and miserable evening. As I approached the presbytery I could see the parish priest putting his car away in the garage, which was on the far side of the church. The house-keeper was away and I let myself into the house. As I went upstairs to my room the phone rang. The nearest telephone was in the parish priest's bedroom, so I put my bag down, opened his bedroom door, stepped in and stopped in great alarm. There was a woman in his bed! I recognised her; she was the parish organist, who didn't live in the parish. I backed out, in great embarrassment and confusion, and went into my bedroom. I closed the door and leant my back on it, shocked. After a few minutes the parish priest came up, went into his bedroom and after a couple of minutes came and knocked on my door. I couldn't open it to face him, so through the closed door he told me that the lady had suffered a nasty accident at the school where she taught, and he had decided that she ought to stay the night!

A number of things happened after that. Relationships became even more tense and stressful; the parish priest gave the house-keeper more and more time off; and his lady friend came to stop for the night more openly and regularly.

It was a dreadful time; the two most unhappy years of my life. I had lived in a secure, supportive community for 12 years and now I was out on my own, so isolated and lonely. There was no one that I could talk to; no local secular clergy I could confide in. The neighbouring parish priest at Peckham Rye was a friend of my parish priest and I had little in common with the Religious communities at Peckham and Brockley. I would not think of telling my parents, because I did not want to shock my devout mother and give a bad impression of the priesthood to my non-Catholic father. Two pieces of spiritual guidance from the seminary rang in my head: don't socialise with the laity and don't ask to be moved, because where you have been placed is where God wants you to be. One thing I had not learnt was how to be assertive; all the emphasis had been upon humble acceptance and obedience. I did not know how to handle the situation and felt totally isolated!

What made things worse was that in the parish and every-where I went visiting – and I gradually visited the whole parish – people said, 'Aren't you lucky to be with such a wonderful priest; he is so good and holy.' Charitably I had to make some positive and agreeable response!

This is a long and painful story and I must stick to the simple basics. I was so unhappy in the house that I could not stand being in that tiny lounge with the parish priest. To avoid him I'd go out of an evening and wander up Nunhead lane and around the litter-strewn streets of the parish, passing happy family homes that I had visited.

The months passed and I became ill. I was having constant headaches and pains in my shoulders. One day off, when I met my mother for a shopping trip in the West End, she asked what was wrong with me, because I was unable to string a sentence together without getting confused. I went to see the doctor – a friend of the parish priest – and he told me to pull myself together and get on with life! I was working hard with the young people and the youth groups; visiting and getting on well with the people, who did not realise that there was anything wrong.

Eventually, after two years, I could take no more. As I was unable privately to use a house phone, I rang Archbishop's House from a public phone box and I got an appointment to see Monsignor Charles Henderson, who was then a vicar-general. He listened kindly to me and I concentrated my account on how the living conditions were affecting my health; I made no mention of the lady. He assured me that I would be moved within the week, and I was.

My new parish priest at Abbey Wood, Michael Collins, had been on the telephone to my previous one, which made him unwelcoming and inhospitable. To get out and away from the Nunhead parish, I had borrowed money and bought a motor-bike. When I arrived at Abbey Wood on my Honda, Father Collins nearly had a fit! He considered the bike and my guitar – which he always called 'that banjo' – very un-priestly. Personally he was very sartorial, wearing, for example, big silver buckles on his shoes. But the good thing was, as time passed, he began to trust me and leave to me more and more of the running of the parish. Although he remained distant, we eventually got on quite well. He was the total opposite to my former parish priest, who would allow me to do nothing. Now I had real responsibility. The Abbey Wood Estate, with the Catholic primary school and its own church of St David's, was placed in my care, and soon youth work began.

My parish priest had heard of my involvement in youth work and asked me to start a parish youth club, to help with the Scouts and Cubs, and to start a Brownie and Guide Company. In the following five years I set these up and other youth groups, including a Folk Club and a Folk Choir called 'The Grove Singers'. Within that time, with the help of some wonderful young people (several of whom tried their vocations), we built an extensive youth provision, with ten youth groups. It was about this time, 1967, that I received a letter from Cardinal Heenan asking me to represent the Catholic Church on the National Association of Youth Clubs. Over the next few years, while continuing with the parish work, I got very involved with the Catholic Youth Service Council and, on their behalf, lectured on youth work to clergy gatherings around the country. Linked to that experience, in 1972, my first two books, on youth work came out.

Very happy in my work, I had, however, taken a personal and spiritual problem with me to Abbey Wood. In my loneliness in the previous parish the only person I had found to talk to (but never about the parish priest's personal life) was a lovely young woman, who did a few jobs in the church on a Saturday. Because of my seminary training, I had rarely spoken, at length, to a young woman of my own age before. I discovered that it is possible to talk to a woman and find a compassionate and sympathetic understanding of who you are and your problems in a way that is different from talking to men. Our chats triggered emotions in me and I found myself wanting to speak to her more often than once a week on a Saturday morning. I started finding excuses for ringing her at work! Then the realisation dawned that I had to break off the relationship, before it led anywhere. I was anxious to avoid acting improperly or being unfaithful to the commitment I had made to celibacy.

When I moved to Abbey Wood there was again no warmth or sharing in the presbytery; conversation was limited to business, and I was always addressed as 'Father'. The atmosphere was not hostile, it just didn't exist at all, as the parish priest led his own private life in his upstairs rooms. Hardly arrived, I caught myself looking around for someone, as I had before, to talk to and be accepted by; just for who I was and not because I was 'Father'. There were several of these relationships and they all remained proper and 'platonic', but nonetheless they were very disturbing for someone who had grown up through adolescence and into manhood kept apart from women. My spiritual life became dominated with the idea that I had a calling to marriage. This was reinforced when I visited homes and families. I would get down on the carpet to play with the children and, again and again, the parents would say, 'You'd make a lovely dad, Father'! The only warmth or affection I was experiencing in daily life was in the families I visited and among the youth of the various clubs and groups.

For seven long years I carried this agonising dilemma in my head. I wanted nothing more than to be a good priest and was anxious to avoid anything that would bring the good name of the priesthood into disrespect. Every day and many times each day I prayed for help, strength and guidance. The spiritual practices of the seminary were not abandoned; I continued, for example, most days, an hour of adoration before the Blessed Sacrament; a practice that I had started, years before, as part of my preparation for Ordination. I went on retreat, on days of recollection and joined the Jesus Caritas Confraternity of priests, to help me. The men in my Jesus Caritas group were terrific priests; Canon Edmund Arbuthnott, Peter Boucher, David Stanley and Jeremiah Cronin. They were a tremendous help and support. We met monthly and I did a monthly 'Day in the Desert' – a day of recollection in solitude. It gradually became clear: I had to seek God's will for me.

Meanwhile two exciting developments were taking place in the parish. The Greater London Council, as it was then, decided to build a new town for 60,000 people, called Thamesmead, on the derelict Arsenal property beside the Thames. Much of it fell within our parish boundaries. There were moves afoot to form a team ministry for the new town, leading to an ecumenical centre and a shared church.

The other development in the parish was what I called the Section System. Having the freedom to develop, pastorally, whatever I liked, I divided the parish up into twelve areas. We found and trained lay leaders for each of these small communities, which we called 'sections'. (The name was taken from the building system at that time being used by the architects and building contractors on Thamesmead.) The leaders' commission was to bring their people together in one another's homes, and find and develop ways of building their own area into a community. I went from area to area – evening after evening – celebrating house Masses. (Later on, when Frank O'Sullivan and Charles Walker arrived in the parish they joined me in this.) It was a very demanding time, but one of the happiest of my ministry. I was trying to put the teaching of the Second Vatican Council on the Church into practice. Only much later did I discover that what we had done in Abbey Wood was to set up 'base communities', as they are called in Latin America. In the 1990s Margaret Hebblethwaite researched our 'Section System' in the parish and included a chapter on it in her book on base communities called *Basic is Beautiful*. So, what with the ten youth groups, the community scheme, the ecumenical project and ordinary parish duties I was run off my feet; which I welcomed, because the long busy days distracted me from my personal conflict.

The first report on the viability of the Thamesmead Ecumenical Project was published in 1967 and signed by Nicholas Stacey (Anglican) and Derek Baker (Congregational). I was thrilled to be invited to be one of the founding members of the team, along with John Morris, the parish priest of Plumstead. My parish priest was not at all interested in ecumenism. In fact, in 1979, as the project got underway in earnest, he was replaced by the dynamic, hard-working Frank O'Sullivan. Frank entered the scene like a whirlwind, full of bounce, exciting new ideas and unbounded enthusiasm. Rather like me, at the time, he didn't know the meaning of the word 'leisure' or the concept of 'time-off'. For the first time I had a parish priest that I could admire, truly respect, learn from and work with. We were joined, some time later, by the admirable Charles Walker, another fine pastoral priest. We made a good team.

There were twelve of us on the Ecumenical Group Ministry. Bishop John Robinson of Woolwich was its first leader, although Revd Alan Bradbury was the executive officer. After a short time, Bishop Robinson was replaced by Bishop David Sheppard, when he came to Woolwich. It was an exciting and challenging time, which I really enjoyed.

In my personal life everything came finally to a head in early September 1970. I had agonised, daily, over what to do. As far as one can ever be, I was one hundred per cent certain that God had called me to the priesthood and I was very happy in my ministry. However, I felt more and more that I was intended to be a married man. I consulted confessors, gradually shared my thoughts with the Caritas group and prayed hard, but the idea would not go away, instead becoming increasingly urgent. I had not been unfaithful to my commitment to celibacy, but the shock I'd had as an innocent and naïve young priest in Nunhead still haunted me and I was frightened that I might do something unworthy of the priesthood. However, I knew for certain that if I left the ministry I would have to go out into the wilderness. I would disappoint my parents, shock some parishioners, be abandoned by fellow priests and be considered, by many, a traitor. Cardinal Heenan had just declared, in the Catholic Press, that any priest who left the active ministry was a Judas!

Then, in September 1970, I went on holiday to Austria with my parents. We stopped at Seefeld and went to Oberammergau for the Passion Play. One sunny afternoon I went for a walk, on my own, on the hillside behind our hotel. I sat on a rock and looked out over Seefeld. I knew that I could not keep deferring the issue; I had to make a decision. I asked myself some basic questions, 'Do I love the priesthood? 'Yes.' 'Do I really believe that I have a vocation to priesthood and to marriage?' 'Yes.' 'Was there a real danger that some time, in the future, I would break my commitment to celibacy and do something scandalous?' 'Yes.' Then I had no alternative, I had to accept myself as I was and leave the active ministry; that was what God was asking me to do. At that moment a wonderful sense of relief swept over me. People sometimes say, 'a weight was lifted from my shoulders'; for me, that afternoon, it was just like that.

On my return with my parents to Dover I went to see the parish priest, Terry Tanner, and he said, 'I can organise a place for you, even for this term, at the local Education College.' I declined the offer and told him that I must not rush into anything and that I could not leave the ecumenical team at a very critical time. Much happened in the following months but I eventually secured a place at Coloma College, West Wickham, for teacher training, to start in September 1971. As things were precarious at Thamesmead and the youth groups in the Abbey Wood parish still depended upon me, I decided to defer entry to the Education Course for another year. I thought that if this was really God's will, the decision would stand the test of time; God does not work in a hurry. So throughout 1971 and the first half of 1972 I gradually prepared to withdraw from my pastoral commitments. I found and trained lay leadership for all the youth groups and for the twelve sections in the parish.

Although I was not leaving over or because of a relationship with anyone, an extraordinary thing happened over the Easter of 1972, just a few months before I left the parish. A group of young people, in their early twenties, wanted me to accompany them to Lourdes to work with the Handicapped Children's Trust. We had little money so we borrowed the parish Ford Transit, drove there, and camped . . . in April! I decided to make it a real pilgrimage, praying for Our Lady's help and guidance in my new life, starting that summer. Thankfully my prayers were answered, rather better than I had expected. While in Lourdes I struck up a friendship with one of our group, Liz Herrington, and was soon feeling quite deeply about her. We continued to see one another that summer and very regularly once I had started at Coloma College. At the end of the course, and just before I started work in September 1973 at the Sandown Court Secondary school, Tunbridge Wells (quite close to the Mark Cross seminary!) we married. We chose to get married at St Pancras Anglican Church in central London, because Liz was a practising Anglican. Some years later, after my dispensation to marry came through, there was a second, convalidation, marriage ceremony, in the Catholic church at Crayford, conducted by my friend, Jerry Cronin.

My parting from my diocese was painful. I had gone to Coloma College, for the year, with the approval of the archbishop, who intended that I should be trained to work at the St John Fisher diocesan school at Purley. In the February I decided that it was my duty to go to see him and explain my situation, genuinely believing he could offer help and guidance. Instead it proved to be one of the most traumatic experiences of my life, the archbishop's tone hostile from the start. Just one example will suffice. When I started to explain my difficulty concerning a vocation to celibacy, the archbishop interrupted with the words, 'What you mean is that you've got a girl pregnant!' The whole interview shocked me beyond words. When I was dismissed, after 35 minutes, I knelt to kiss his ring and he said, 'Come back and see me, Father, at the end of the course; I will pray for you.' In a complete daze I returned to my digs at West Wickham and collapsed on the floor, shaken rigid. No one will ever know the desolation I felt. I had given the best years of my life to the Church, making real sacrifices to do so, yet now felt rejected by it. And that rejection was to continue. When the end of the course came, I wrote to Archbishop Cowderoy, as I had promised I would, and I received a five-line dismissive letter telling me to get in touch with the diocesan chancellor if I wanted to be laicised. In that fashion, my 22 years (as seminarian and priest) with the diocese bluntly ended. No one came near; no one made contact. There was no further contact of any kind; it was as though I had never existed.

Fortunately my first employer was not bothered about a reference. When I was offered the job of Youth Tutor at the Sandown Court School, Tunbridge Wells – about the time of this final letter – the headteacher told me that he and the HMI inspector, who had interviewed me, had given me the job because they had been impressed by the moral courage I had displayed in following my conscience.

That summer, as soon as I had taken my final exams at Coloma College, I went to work for Kevin Mayhew and Joan McCrimmon at their publishing house in Great Wakering. Although they did not get on – and the company eventually split apart – they were both extremely kind and supportive. They provided me with a place to stay and my first waged income.

Reflecting now on the past I appreciate that it wasn't an issue easy for my colleagues and friends in the priesthood to handle at that time. It was particularly hard on Jeremiah Cronin, my best friend, with whom I had shared holidays, projects and good times together. Looking back I was so full of coping with my own problems and settling into secular life that I didn't appreciate how hard it was for him, and others, to come to terms with my departure.

Lay friends were splendid; we had many cards and presents sent to our little home when the news got back to Abbey Wood that we had married. Our local parish priest at Mayfield, Eric Flood, was very welcoming and within weeks he had me playing the guitar and getting the children singing at Sunday Mass. But it was not easy to settle into a totally new way of life and some hostility continued. That Christmas, 1973, I spent my first real complete Christmas with my parents and family for 22 years. Liz and I had a wonderful time; it was only spoilt by one disturbing event. When we went, as a family, to Midnight Mass, the curate came up to me, as we were entering the church and, without any greeting said, 'If you present yourself for Holy Communion tonight we will refuse you'! So, to avoid a fuss, I did not receive Holy Communion that Christmas night in the parish church where I had been baptised.

My first job at the Sandown Court Secondary was ideal for me, as it combined youth work and RE teaching. Liz worked nearby at the Midland Bank in Tunbridge Wells. After three years there I approached the Diocesan Education authorities and asked if I might apply for a post in a Catholic secondary school. Monsignor Mahoney, of the Schools Commission, wrote back telling me that I would never be employed in the Southwark Archdiocese. So instead I accepted an invitation by Kevin Mayhew to join his publishing house in Essex, having in 1971 been one of a panel of liturgical editors – including Stephen Dean, Michael Buckley, Kevin Donovan and Mark Searle – involved in the launch of a new international liturgical journal called *Christian Celebration*. After I married, Kevin Mayhew asked me to act as executive editor, and Liz and I ran the magazine – apart from the printing and so forth – from our little home in Crowborough.

We moved house, in 1976, to Great Wakering, near Southend-on-Sea, to work for Mayhew–McCrimmon, but not before we had a little domestic tragedy. Eighteen months after we commenced married life, Liz became pregnant and there was great joy all round. This turned to sadness when, three months later, the baby died in the womb, which led to a debilitating illness for Liz. Thankfully we had our first-born, Helena, before we moved to Great Wakering; next came Louise and then Angela. We thought our little family was complete, but unexpectedly – and very happily – Thomas arrived on the scene in 1985.

When Bishop Michael Bowen was appointed to Southwark I felt that I could now approach Archbishop's House about a dispensation without fear of rejection. It was a great relief to be warmly received by the archbishop, who personally made me a cup of tea and listened sympathetically to my request and the reasons for it. I told him that I was utterly convinced of my vocation to the priesthood and equally convinced of a vocation to marriage; and that I could not see that the two vocations clashed or were mutually exclusive. He accepted everything that I had to say and asked me simply to write out in my application what I sincerely believed. This I did in October 1977, asking for a dispensation from canon 132 (as it was at that time). Eventually, on 16 March 1978, I received a very kind letter from Archbishop Bowen informing me that the dispensation to marry – on the usual terms – had been granted. At no point or time was the term 'laicisation' used or mention made of 'returning to the lay state'.

Through a series of unfortunate events at Mayhew–McCrimmon – a long story in itself – I found myself unemployed in 1978, with firsthand experience of the dole queue! It caused severe financial problems for the family for some time. I poured myself into research and compilation of what was to prove to be my best-known book, *Quotes and Anecdotes for Preachers and Teachers*. My reasoning was, if I can't preach at least I can help those who can. It was published in 1979 and led to a series of books offering aids and support to busy pastoral priests and teachers. Eventually, I came to work, once again, for Kevin Mayhew, who had split away from Joan McCrimmon and her business at Great Wakering. As his Sales Director I toured the country and saw the company's sales outlets increase substantially. When Kevin moved the publishing company from Westcliff-on-Sea, to East Anglia, I left, as I didn't want to move my family from Great Wakering, with its excellent local Catholic school, where we were all settled.

Great Wakering has its own chapel-of-ease, St Edmund's, with, until recently, a Mass at the weekend. From soon after our arrival in the large village, I was entrusted by Father Pat Taylor with the care of the church and that pastoral area within the parish of Shoebury-ness. After a few years Bishop Thomas McMahon confirmed me as a Pastoral Lay Assistant – the first to be appointed in the Brentwood Diocese. I have served now for over 20 years as a PLA, taking Holy Communion to the sick, visiting, and organising worship and social events with the other five churches in the village. For years I was the chairman of Churches Together in Wakering. The Bishop of Brentwood has been wonderful in his support, allowing me to do everything possible within the present framework.

When the post of Head of the RE Department became available at St Bernard's High School for Girls, at Westcliff-on-Sea, I received the wholehearted support of the priests of the deanery; which, thankfully, I have continued to enjoy. Every year, for example, they ask me to train the Eucharistic Ministers for the Deanery. What has helped in my gradual return to acceptance in the life of the Church has been the stream of pastoral books for priests and teachers, and books on spirituality and prayer that have appeared. There have been two special highlights, where my books are concerned. The first was when I was asked by the Hierarchy of Hungary to permit them to translate *Through the Year with Pope John Paul* and use it for the papal visit to Hungary in the summer of 1991. Father Lazio, the secretary of the Bishops' Conference sent me a copy in the autumn, signed for me by the pope. The other highlight was when St Paul Publications presented me with the Chinese edition of *Gateway to the Trinity* for sale in Taiwan!

There was a red-letter day for our whole family in December 1983 when Archbishop Bowen went to Dover and awarded my mother the Bene Merenti medal for 50 years of humble service to her parish; 50 years of weekly church-cleaning, brass polishing, coffee-making and such like. We were so proud of her. Sadly only months later my father was left desolately alone.

I am happy to say that, as retirement approaches, my story has come almost full circle. Priests and religious are once again regular visitors to our home, which also has an open door to local neighbours and friends. I serve the diocese as the Director of the Catholic Certificate of Religious Studies and as an Ofsted inspector of RE, while, at present, serving as a Head of RE and as a Pastoral Lay Assistant in my parish. My wife, who became a Catholic in 1993, is as involved in the local parish community as my mother was. My eldest daughter, Helena, teaches in a local Catholic primary school; my second daughter, Louise, serves the community as a special baby-care nurse. Angela, my third daughter, took a gap year out of her education, three years ago, to work for the diocese of Brentwood as a youth leader at Walsingham House, the Diocesan Youth Centre. She is currently studying for her Degree in Podiatry. Thomas is a catechist in our parish, and also very involved with the Brentwood Youth Service. He is hoping to go to university to study computer sciences. I am immensely proud of my family and their achievements.

Just one last story. I have never hidden from anyone my background and personal history; I have never had cause to, nor had any doubt that I did the right thing. Because I have tried to be open with people, I have attracted questions. Not so much about my personal story, but about the strange inconsistency and apparent lack of justice in the institutional Church. 'How,' people frequently ask, 'can the Church allow former Anglican married vicars to live and work in parishes as married Catholic priests and not allow you, who have a priestly vocation, to serve?' I assure people that I have no problem about the former Anglicans; in fact I work regularly with four excellent married priests, with their families, in our local deanery. But I have never found a satisfactory answer to the question. It was because of this that I wrote, in June 1997, to Cardinal Basil Hume asking him what reply I should give to people. He replied kindly, inviting me to go up to see him at Archbishop's house, Westminster.

When the visit took place the Cardinal greeted me at the door, took me up to his private study and made us both a cup of tea – he recommended the ginger-nut biscuits! Then he sat back and encouraged me to tell my story. He was an excellent and sympathetic listener. At one point he commented, 'I wish the Holy Father was here, to hear what you have to say.' He asked a few questions and then said, 'I have no doubt that you have a vocation to the priesthood, and to marriage, but you know how things are. There's little that I can do. I could take a petition with me to Rome, when I go in February.' He warmed to the idea and told me that he was meeting Cardinal Ratzinger himself and would personally present my petition to him requesting that I be allowed to return to priestly duties. 'However,' the Cardinal said, 'I don't want you to get your hopes up. You know what Rome is like. But I promise to try, and I will support your application with my own recommendation. The Church should never stand in the way of God's will, which seems apparent to me in this case.' He asked if my bishop would want me to work in the Brentwood diocese if the petition were granted. When I affirmed that he would, he said, 'That's a pity, I'd snap you up here, if you were available.' I left with a spring in my step, not so much because I was full of hope – indeed, I had my doubts – but because the highest Church authority in England and Wales had listened kindly to me and believed me.

The petition was written and sent to Cardinal Hume. I heard no more until May 1998. The Cardinal wrote on the 21st to say, 'I am afraid the authorities in Rome reacted rather as I expected. Nonetheless it is disappointing for you, and indeed for us. I do think that yours was a special case.' It was, sadly, the answer I too was expecting, but for me, in a sense, it laid everything finally to rest. I had hoped, even expected, for many years, to be able to return one day to the practice of the vocation to which I had been called. Now, I no longer look for that day or expect it to come. I am content to keep on trying to do my best for my wife and family, my local parish and diocese.

Postscript

Every Christian celebration involves faith, hope and love; and a Ruby Anniversary of Priesthood is no different. It is faith that prompts and gives purpose, love that unites and hope that gives promise. Faith, deep faith, underlies everything that is written in this book. There can be no doubting the love of God and neighbour revealed here. And this Class of '63 has been unusual, in clerical circles, in maintaining an annual reunion. When the time comes they hope to be together, in good health, to celebrate their Golden Jubilee. They also hope that there will be priests to follow in their footsteps.

This book shows clearly how the life of the secular priest has changed, considerably, over the past forty years. The first story tells of the small community of priests, happily living and working together, in the Woolwich parish. While this was not, as the last story recounts, everyone's experience, at least it was rare, then, for a secular priest to be alone; living with others was the norm. It is now, for the first time in history, the exception; most secular priests live alone. This can make a life dedicated to celibacy even harder than it once was. The laity, whose generous support has been noted and appreciated several times in these pages, can do much not just to help 'Father' in ministries and parish duties but also, as it is put these days, 'to be there for him'. At the end of the day it is not the priest who builds a parish into a community, but the people. The more parishioners realise and appreciate that they are the Church, the more they will take responsibility for the welfare of their priests. And the more a parish is a real community, a family of Christ's faithful people, the more the secular priest will feel 'at home' and valued, and the less he will feel isolated and alone.

Each contributor rejoiced in the liturgical changes of the Second Vatican Council, but maybe the devotional prayer-life of our communities is not what it once was when these stories began. From one of the retired priests contributing to this book comes a simple appeal to all priests to encourage their people to develop their prayer-life. If Catholics want to have priests in their parishes in 40 years time, then now is the time to build outward-looking, caring communities; the time to build up the prayer-life of our families and each parish community, and the time to cherish and take good care, in every way, of our secular priests.